D1730534

HONG KONG

香　港

GOLD

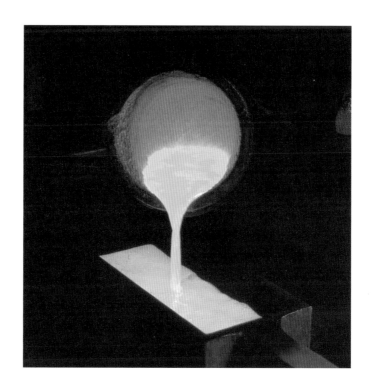

金

THE HONG KONG
GOLD MARKET

香 港 金 市 錄

First published in Great Britain in 1995 by
Rosendale Press Limited
Premier House, 10 Greycoat Place
London SW1P 1SB

ISBN 1 872 803 31 8

Printed in Hong Kong by Equity Financial Press Limited

British Library Cataloguing in Publication Data
A catalogue record for the book is available from the British Library.

1995年英國第一版
Rosendale Press Limited 出版
Premier House, 10 Greycoat Place
London SW1P 1SB

國際統一書號：ISBN 1 872 803 31 8

香港安業財經植字有限公司承印

本書已列入英國圖書館出版資料目錄
目錄卡存於大英圖書館，可供參閱。

THE HONG KONG GOLD MARKET

香 港 金 市 錄

ROBERT SITT

薛俊豪編著

ROSENDALE PRESS

CONTENTS 目錄

CONTENTS (con't) 目錄 (續)

HISTORY 歷史

HONG KONG IN THE 1950s
一九五零年代的香港

The Hong Kong gold market has grown to a status of international importance since the mid 1970s. It is now a vital component in the world's gold trading market.

Gold trading in Hong Kong started as early as 1910 when a company was incorporated by a small group of money changers and traders. The name of the company was "The Gold and Silver Exchange Company" and the principal business was to trade in gold and silver among the traders themselves. In the following few years, the management of the company continued moving forward to expand the trading activities and, in 1918, the name of the company was changed to "The Chinese Gold & Silver Exchange Society" ("the Exchange"). Subsequently, the Exchange made various proposals to the Government and was eventually given permission by the authority to offer facilities to the public for trading in gold bullion. The fineness of the bars was 990 parts per 1,000 fine gold and the Exchange was effectively the first gold trading exchange established in the world.

香港黃金市場的國際地位自七零年代中起日漸提升，時至今日，在全球黃金買賣網中香港更是不可或缺的一環。

在香港買賣黃金的歷史可追溯至1910年。當時一群錢幣找換商及買賣商成立了「金銀貿易公司」，主要為方便彼此間買賣黃金和白銀。隨後數年，這家公司的買賣活動不斷擴展，更於1918年易名為「金銀業貿易場」（「貿易場」）。貿易場向政府作出多項建議，最後取得政府許可，向公眾提供買賣黃金的設施，所買賣的黃金成色達千分之九百九十。所以實際上這個貿易場是全球首個黃金交易所。

In 1947, two years after the Japanese occupation (1941-1945) of Hong Kong, the Importation and Exportation of Gold (Prohibition) Regulation was enacted in compliance with the exchange control regulation in the Sterling Area. Buying and selling gold bullion was prohibited under the new legislation and trading in the Exchange was suspended. After a careful review, the Government agreed later in the year that the Exchange could resume trading in industrial gold of 945 fine instead of gold bullion of 990 fine.

The Inauguration of the Exchange Building (1935)　　貿易場新廈開幕典禮（1935）

為配合在英鎊區實行的外滙管制，香港於1947年，即日治時期（1941－45）結束後兩年，制訂了黃金進出口（禁止）規例。在新規例下，黃金買賣被禁止，因此在貿易場進行的交易亦要暫停。政府在進行詳細檢討後，於同年同意貿易場可恢復買賣成色由990調低至945的工業用黃金。

In view of this development, the Hongkong-Macau gold trade was subsequently established. The business was undertaken exclusively by Mount Trading (owned jointly by Jardine Matheson and Samuel Montagu), Commercial Investment (a subsidiary of Wheelock Marden) and Premex (with major shareholders in Switzerland and Panama). Special licences were granted to these three companies by the Government to import gold, mainly from London, into Hong Kong for transhipment and sale to Macau.

The gold business in Macau was handled by Wong On Hong (owned by Dr Cheng Yu Tung of Chow Tai Fook) under a franchise granted by the Portuguese Government. The quantity of gold imported into Macau was relatively substantial despite the small population in the tiny Portuguese colony. It was generally acknowledged that after the metal was sold to traders in Macau, the bulk of the quantity was shipped back to Hong Kong through a network of unofficial channels to take advantage of the price differential.

在這種情況下，香港－澳門的黃金貿易便逐步建立起來，業務由民達公司（怡和及英國萬達基的合營公司）、豐業投資（會德豐的附屬機構）及培民斯（主要股東在瑞士及巴拿馬）壟斷經營。香港政府發出特別牌照予這三家公司，主要從倫敦輸入黃金，然後轉運往澳門出售。

澳門的黃金買賣由王安行（由周大福的鄭裕彤博士擁有）按葡國政府頒授的專營權經營。雖然當時澳門人口稀少，但黃金進口量相當大，一般人都相信黃金在售給澳門買賣商後，大部分透過非正式途徑運回香港出售，賺取差價。

Member Certificate of the Exchange (1930)
貿易場的行員證書（1930）

The Hongkong-Macau trade lasted for twenty-seven years until January 1974 when the gold market in Hong Kong was liberalized following the dissolution of the Sterling Area in 1972. This development, coupled with the abolition of exchange controls, allowed international trading in gold to commence in Hong Kong. Aided by the telecommunication infrastructure already developed and facilities available in the financial community, the Hong Kong gold market rapidly gained international recognition. Both the volume of business and the number of counterparties increased steadily in the following years.

香港－澳門的黃金貿易維持了二十七年，直至1974年才終止。繼英鎊區制度於1972年解體後，黃金便由1974年1月起恢復在香港自由買賣。在解除外滙管制的配合下，香港開始了國際黃金買賣，再輔以完善的通訊基本建設以及金融市場的設施，香港的黃金市場很快便在國際間建立地位。自此之後，黃金買賣和參與者的數目多年來一直有增無減。

By the late 1970s, the loco London gold market was firmly established in Hong Kong with the physical presence of practically all the major bullion houses and banks in the world. They included Johnson Matthey, Mocatta, N. M. Rothschild & Sons, Samuel Montagu, Sharps Pixley, Derby and Engelhard from London; Credit Suisse, SBC and UBS from Switzerland; Deutsche Bank and Dresdner Bank from Germany; Bache Securities, Bank of America, Bank of Boston, Bank of Nova Scotia, Bankers Trust, Citibank, Dean Witter Reynolds, Merrill Lynch, Morgan Guaranty Trust, Republic National Bank of New York, Shearson Lehman Brothers, Shun Loong Bear Stearns and Wardley-Acli from North America.

Additionally, several international bullion brokers set up offices in Hong Kong to provide dealing prices from Europe. Reuters and AP Dow Jones also extended their operation in the territory to supply various dealing equipment required for the growing business.

到七零年代終，本地倫敦金市場已在香港奠定穩固基礎，大部分世界主要的金商及金業銀行亦相繼在香港開設辦事處，其中包括倫敦的莊信萬豐、慕加達、羅富齊父子、萬達基、金多利、打比及英高克；瑞士的瑞士信貸銀行、瑞士銀行及瑞士聯合銀行；德國的德意志銀行及捷能銀行；北美洲的培基證券、美國銀行、波士頓銀行、加拿大豐業銀行、美國信孚銀行、萬國寶通銀行、添惠證券、美林集團、摩根信託、利寶銀行、雷曼兄弟、順隆美亞及獲多利億順。

此外，若干國際黃金經紀行均在香港設立辦事處提供歐洲黃金買賣盤價。路透社及美聯社亦擴展在香港的業務，為這個不斷發展的行業提供各類所需的買賣系統。

The successful development of loco London gold trading in Hong Kong complemented the tael gold business conducted on the Exchange. The level of activities greatly increased in the following few years and a record high daily turnover of nearly 4,000,000 ounces on the Exchange and in the loco London market was reached in 1981. A substantial amount of interest in trading in gold was generated from a wide cross-section of local people in Hong Kong ranging from traders and manufacturers to investors and speculators.

本地倫敦金市場成功在香港發展,正好與貿易場的黃金買賣相輔相成。在之後的數年間,香港的黃金買賣業務大幅提升;至1981年,貿易場及本地倫敦金市場的交投量更創下每天近4,000,000盎司的高紀錄。不少香港人對買賣黃金的興趣相當濃厚,包括買賣商、製造商以至投資者及投機人士。

Mase Westpac Hong Kong Limited (1980s)　　美思太平洋香港有限公司（1980年代）

In April 1984, the Hong Kong Bullion Dealers Club (HKBDC) was founded with the prime objective of developing professional ethics and conduct of bullion dealing in Hong Kong. Mr Robert Sitt (Samuel Montagu Hong Kong) was elected President while Mr Dick Gazmararian (Mocatta Hong Kong) and Mr Yip Lai Shing (Sun Hung Kai Securities) were elected First and Second Vice President respectively. To help strengthening the relationship between Hong Kong and other major bullion markets, senior members of the bullion industry in the world were appointed Honorary Presidents of the Club. They included Mr Robert Fell (Commissioner for Securities & Commodities Trading, Hong Kong), the Late Dr Woo Hon Fai (President, Chinese Gold & Silver Exchange Society, Hong Kong), Mr Rudolf K. Schriber (Credit Suisse, Zurich), Mr Fritz Plass (Deutsche Bank, Frankfurt), Mr Robert Guy (N. M. Rothschild & Sons, London) and Dr Henry Jarecki (Mocatta Metals Corporation, New York).

1984年4月，香港黃金交易員協會成立，其主要目的在於培養香港黃金交易從業員的專業操守。萬達基執行董事薛俊豪先生獲選為該會主席，第一及第二副主席分別由慕加達執行董事加薩馬蘭先生及新鴻基證券執行董事葉黎成先生擔任。為協助加強香港與其他主要黃金市場的聯繫，該會更禮聘世界黃金業知名人士擔任名譽主席，包括香港證券及商品交易監理專員霍禮義先生、金銀業貿易場理事長胡漢輝博士（已故）、瑞士信貸銀行史齊博先生、德國德意志銀行柏尼斯先生、英國羅富齊父子基亞先生，及美國慕加達翟洛其博士。

The Inauguration of HKBDC (1984)　　香港黃金交易員協會成立典禮（1984）

The world gold market has stagnated gradually since the mid 1980s subsequent to the deflationary policy and fiscal measures adopted by the G-7 nations. The volume of business in Hong Kong has also shrunk drastically in the past 10 years. Nonetheless, confidence in the bullion industry has been returning lately and major international markets are staging a comeback. The time is opportune to review the existing structure of the gold market in Hong Kong.

由於七大工業國採取壓抑通脹及緊縮貨幣政策，自八十年代中開始，世界黃金市場轉趨呆滯。香港的黃金買賣在過去十年間亦大幅縮減。雖然如此，市場最近已逐漸恢復對黃金的信心，主要國際市場亦開始出現復甦跡象，所以現在是檢討香港金市架構的最適當時候。

CURRENT STATUS 現況

HONG KONG IN THE 1990s
一九九零年代的香港

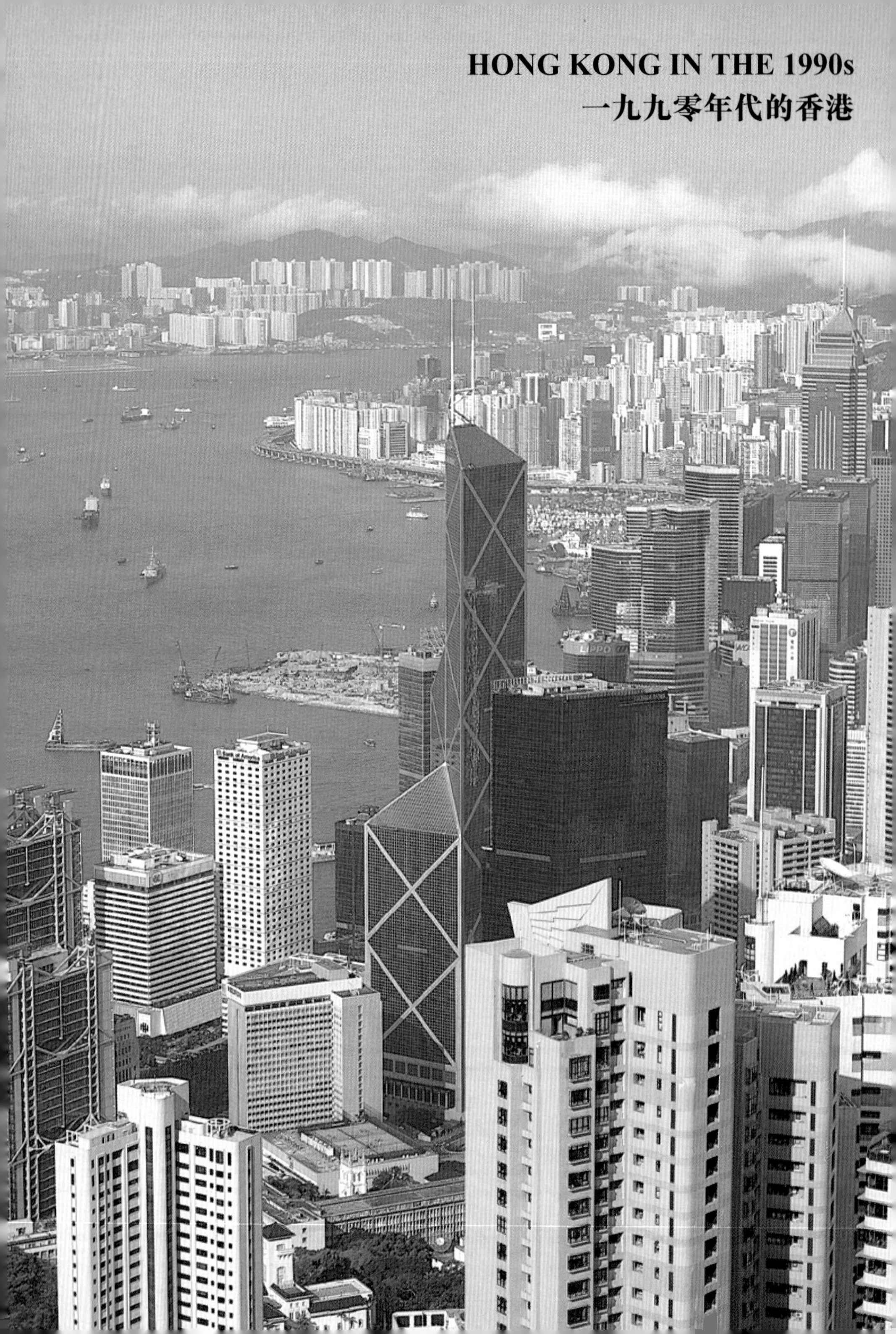

THE TRADING MARKET

交 易 市 場

THE CHINESE GOLD & SILVER EXCHANGE SOCIETY 金銀業貿易場

The Chinese Gold & Silver Exchange Society ("The Exchange"), established in 1918, is predominantly Chinese and employs Chinese weights and measures and local currency as trading units. The Exchange is also known as "Kam Ngan Exchange" which is the translation of "Gold and Silver Exchange". Trading is conducted under an open outcry system and prices are expressed in Hong Kong dollars per tael (1.20337 troy ounces) of gold of 990 fine. Each contract covers 20 five-tael bars and transactions concluded are for same day settlement which can be deferred at the discretion of buyers or sellers subject to the payment or receipt of a Carried Over Charge (COC).

The COC rate normally fluctuates in accordance with the prevailing physical supply and demand for tael bars and is fixed daily at the Exchange at 11:00 hours (10:00 hours on Saturdays). The rate is fixed in HK$ per ten taels.

金銀業貿易場（「貿易場」）於1918年成立，主要由華人參與買賣，採用中國量重方法以港元作價。所有買賣均以公開喊價方式進行，買賣以兩（1.20337 金衡盎司）為單位，金條成色為 990。每份合約為二十條五兩條，於買賣當日交收結算，但在買方或賣方同意收取或支付倉費後，可以遞延結算。

倉費的議定一般按現貨兩條的供求量而上落，並於每天上午11時（星期六為10時）在貿易場議定。倉費按每十兩以港元計算。

The COC rates are classified under five grades, each grade with a maximum limit as detailed below:

First Grade	–	up to 10.8% per annum
Second Grade	–	up to 14.4% per annum
Third Grade	–	up to 18.0% per annum
Fourth Grade	–	up to 21.6% per annum
Fifth Grade	–	up to 25.2% per annum

When there is a shortage of physical tael bars to meet the demand, the COC rate is fixed at a level at which buyers agree to roll over the open positions by receiving the respective amount of COC for the day. Should demand continue to exceed supply after COC has reached the maximum limit for the First Grade for three consecutive days, the rate will be increased on the fourth day to the Second Grade. If supply remains short, the rate will be increased to the Third Grade and so on until the Fifth Grade maximum limit is fixed.

倉費分為五級，每級的最高限額如下：

一級	—	最高可達年息10.8%
二級	—	最高可達年息14.4%
三級	—	最高可達年息18.0%
四級	—	最高可達年息21.6%
五級	—	最高可達年息25.2%

如現貨兩條供不應求，倉費將定於買家同意以收取當天所議定的倉費（高息）來滾計未清倉盤的水平。倘若求過於供的情況不變，而一級倉費的最高限額持續三天，則倉費會在第四天升至二級。如同樣的情況再持續，則倉費會升至三級，如此類推，一直至第五級的最高限額。

According to past experience, physical tael bars are always available when the Fifth Grade maximum limit becomes effective. The reverse rates of COC are applicable when the supply of tael bars exceeds demand. Carried Over Charge is not payable until the deal is closed.

In the case of settlement being deferred, the maturity date is not specified. Members are permitted to hold a net open

按照以往的經驗，現貨兩條在倉費升至五級的最高限額時必會有足夠供應。在同一制度下，如現貨兩條供過於求，倉費會以相反方向議定（低息）。議定倉費在交易完成後繳付。

在遞延結算的情況下，一般是不會訂明到期日的。會員的戶口內最多可持有2,500兩未平倉合約淨額，但如超出限額，

The Trading Hall of the "Exchange"　貿易場的交易大堂

position of up to 2,500 taels each in their accounts. Should the limit be exceeded, an initial margin of HK$40,000 (non-interest bearing) per contract has to be deposited with the Exchange.

In order to facilitate trading, some members of the Exchange deal among themselves for more than 2,500 taels without depositing the required initial margin with the Exchange. This practice is currently acceptable although members are taking credit risks for the quantity exceeding 2,500 taels. Officially, the risk can be eliminated by transferring the deals to the Exchange but such a course of action would adversely affect working relationships with other members.

The Exchange fixes daily the official clearing price for the morning and afternoon session at 11:30 and 16:00 hours respectively (only one fixing at 10:30 hours on Saturdays). All open positions are marked to market accordingly and variation margin is called and paid.

則每份合約須在貿易場存有40,000港元的基本保證金（不計利息）。

為方便交收，會員買賣的數量有時超逾2,500両，但卻沒有在貿易場存入規定的基本保證金。這種做法現在已頗被接受，但會員本身則要承受超額量的價格保付風險。正式來說，把超額量轉予貿易場可除去這個風險，不過這種做法會影響與其他會員的貿易關係。

貿易場每天在上午11時30分及下午4時定出上午及下午的正式結算價（星期六只有一次定價，在上午10時30分進行），所有未平倉盤均以結算價對數，補交價格變動保證金給予對方。

In the event of drastic price movements, the President of the Exchange has the right to suspend trading on the floor when the price movement exceeds HK$500 per tael (either way) compared to the official clearing price fixed at the previous session. All outstanding deals must be closed with the maximum profit or loss of HK$50,000 per contract for immediately settlement. Thereafter, trading will resume with the normal margin calls. Under this practice, the Exchange has been able to conduct gold trading without any major financial problem since its establishment.

The Black Touchstone Testing Process　　磨金石檢驗両條成色步驟

如價格大幅波動而超逾前定的正式結算價每両500港元時，貿易場理事長有權暫停場內交易。這時所有未完成的合約均須成交，每份合約最高以賺/蝕50,000港元為限。之後，交易便回復正常，保證金維持不變。在這個機制下，貿易場自成立以來均能順利進行黃金買賣，並無遇到重大財務問題。

There are 192 members on the Exchange of whom 31 are acceptable melters of tael bars. The fineness and weight of the bars produced by these melters are checked by the Exchange. The black touchstone process is employed for testing of the fineness and if the bars conform to the required standard they are stamped with the official chop of the Exchange. Currently, Chow Sang Sang, Hing Fung, King Fook, Lee Cheong, Po Sang Bank and Sun Hung Kai are the leading producers.

The Exchange is recognized by the Hong Kong Government as a semi-official organization for gold trading but its operation is completely independent without any Government interference or supervision. In view of its excellent track record for the past seven decades, the trading practice adopted by the Exchange is well accepted by traders, jewellery manufacturers, hoarders and speculators in Asia. Tael gold bars bearing the official chop of the Exchange are recognized in the region as Hong Kong Good Delivery bars.

貿易場共有192名行員，其中31名為認許金條熔鑄商。由這些熔鑄商生產的黃金，貿易場會以磨金石方法檢驗其成色及重量，符合標準的金條，貿易場會蓋上正式印鑑。目前香港的金條主要是由周生生、慶豐、景福、利昌、寶生銀行及新鴻基等生產。

雖然在黃金買賣方面，貿易場是香港政府承認的機構，但其運作則完全不受政府干預或監管。過去七十多年來，貿易場的營運紀錄均十分良好，其買賣方式因此廣獲亞洲的交易商、金飾製造商、長線投資者及投機人士接受，印有貿易場正式印鑑的兩條在亞洲被視為香港認許金條。

The Executive and Supervisory Committee of the Exchange comprises 21 members. Mr Henry Wu King Cheong (Lee Cheong) is the current President. Mr Fung Chi Kin (Yue Seng) and Mr Raymond Chan Fat Chu (Hing Fung) are the Vice Chairmen. Mr Siu Kwan Luen (Wai Chong) is the Chairman of the Supervisory Committee. Dr Ho Sin Hang, Dr Ho Tim, Mr Wu Jieh Yee and Mr Zee Kwok Kung are the Honorary Permanent Presidents.

The 1995 Executive Committee Members of the Exchange   1995年度貿易場理監事

貿易場現時共有21名理監事,胡經昌先生(利昌)為現任理事長,馮志堅先生(裕生)及陳發柱先生(慶豐)為副理事長。蕭坤鑾先生(惠昶)則為監事長。何善衡博士、何添博士、伍潔宜先生及徐國炯先生為永遠名譽會長。

THE GOLD FUTURES MARKET　期金市場

Pursuing a policy to develop Hong Kong as a regional financial centre, the Hong Kong Government enacted the Commodities Trading Ordinance in 1976. The Hong Kong Commodity Exchange (HKCE) was incorporated in 1977 following the liberalization of commodity futures trading. Raw sugar, raw cotton and soybeans futures were traded during the first phase of the operation.

為發展香港成為亞太區金融中心，香港政府於1976年訂立商品交易條例，而香港商品交易所在開放商品期貨買賣後，於1977年成立，初期僅提供設施買賣原糖、原棉及黃豆期貨。

The Hong Kong Futures Exchange　　香港期貨交易所

In 1980, the scope of activities of HKCE was widened to include gold futures trading. Business is conducted under an open outcry system. Each contract covers 100 troy ounces and the original margin required for each contract is US$1,500. Prices are quoted in US dollars per troy ounce and price changes are registered in multiples of US$10 per contract. If the price movement exceeds US$40 per troy ounce above or below the settlement price established at the close of the preceding market day, trading will be suspended for 30 minutes for special margin calls. Thereafter, trading will resume without limits until the close of the day.

In fulfilment of every contract, the seller must deliver to the buyer 100 troy ounces (5% more or less) of Good Delivery gold bars of 995 fine or better. The weight of each bar can be 100 troy ounces, 50 troy ounces or one kilo. Delivery can be made at the seller's option during any business day from the 23rd day to the last working day of the month specified in the contract.

1980年，商品交易所的業務範圍有所擴展，開始買賣黃金期貨。買賣是以公開喊價方式進行。每份合約是以100金衡益司為單位，保證金為每份合約1,500美元，以每金衡益司美元定價。每份合約的價格變動為10美元或其倍數，倘若每金衡益司價格的變動超過上一個交易日收市結算價40美元，買賣即暫停30分鐘以補交額外保證金。之後，買賣將會恢復，直至當天收市也不設任何價格變動的限制。

在完成每份合約時，賣方必須交付100金衡益司（最多有5%增減差額）國際認許金條予買方，純度最少是995，而重量可選擇每條100金衡益司、50金衡益司或1公斤。交付可於該月23日至最後交易日，按賣方於合約指明的日期進行。

HKCE changed its name to Hong Kong Futures Exchange in 1985 but the performance of gold futures trading has been below expectation. On the other hand, traders and speculators are keen to trade on the New York Mercantile Exchange COMEX Division in New York and the volume of business conducted by night operators in Hong Kong has been fairly substantial. This is primarily due to greater price activity during New York market hours.

The Trading Ring of the COMEX Division, New York　　紐約期貨交易所的交易大堂

商品交易所於1985年轉名為香港期貨交易所，但黃金期貨買賣一般的表現都未如理想。另一方面，交易商及投機者夜間在紐約期貨交易所進行買賣的數量卻很大，主要是因為紐約市場較為活躍。

THE LOCO LONDON GOLD MARKET
本地倫敦金市場

The trading of gold in the London market has a long history of three centuries but Gold Fixing was only formalized after the first World War in 1919. The system of Fixing originated from the London silver market and the concept is to provide market users throughout the world with the opportunity to buy and sell gold at a single quoted price. The Fixings take place twice daily at 10:30 and 15:00 hours in the City of London with the participation of the following five Fixing Members:

> Deutsche Bank Sharps Pixley
> Midland Bank PLC
> N. M. Rothschild & Sons Limited
> Republic National Bank of New York
> Standard Chartered Bank, Mocatta Group

黃金買賣在倫敦已有三個世紀的歷史，但倫敦議價的制度則在第一次世界大戰後，於1919年始正式實行。這個制度源於倫敦的白銀市場，其目的是使全球的市場參與者能以單一報價買賣黃金。議價每天上午10時30分及下午3時由以下五家金商於倫敦會商定出：

> 德意志銀行－金多利
> 米特蘭銀行
> 羅富齊父子
> 美國利寶銀行
> 標準渣打銀行－慕加達

The procedure of the Fixing is described by the London Bullion Market Association (LBMA) as follows:

"Each member of the Fixing sends a representative who maintains telephone contact with his dealing room. The Chairman of the Fixing, traditionally the representative of N. M. Rothschild & Sons Limited, announces an opening price which is reported back to the dealing rooms. They in turn relay this price to their customers, and, on the basis of orders received, instruct their representative to declare as a

The Gold Fixing Room of LBMA　　倫敦金市協會的議價室

議價程序按倫敦金市協會所述如下：

「每家金商派出一位代表與其公司的盤房保持電話聯絡，由會商議價的主席（一向為羅富齊父子有限公司的代表）報出開市價，各代表隨即將開市價通知盤房，向其客戶報價，而

buyer or seller. Provided both buying and selling interests are declared, members are then asked to state the number of bars in which they wish to trade.

"If at the opening price there is either no buying or no selling, or if the size for the buying and selling does not balance, the same procedure is followed again at higher or lower prices until a balance is achieved. At this moment the Chairman announces that the price is 'Fixed'. Exceptionally a pro-rata settlement may be necessary.

"A feature of the London Fixing is that customers may be kept advised of price changes throughout a Fixing meeting, and may alter their instructions at any time until the price is Fixed. To ensure that a member can communicate such alteration, his representative has a small flag which he raises and, as long as any flag is raised, the Chairman may not declare the price fixed."

按所收到的買賣盤，代表宣告以該價格買入或沽出。在該價格一經宣布有買家及賣家後，各代表便須報出其擬買賣的金條數量。

「倘報出開市價後並無買家或賣家，或倘買入及沽出的數量不平衡，則須重新按相同程序開出較高或較低的價格，直到買賣數量取得平衡為止。屆時主席便會宣布該價格為'議定價'。在若干情況下，可能需要按比例交收。

「倫敦議價的一項特色是客戶可以得知議價進行中的價格變動，及可隨時更改其指示，直到價格議定為止。為確保能及時傳達更改指示，各代表均手持小旗，只要有任何小旗舉起，主席便不得宣布該價格為議定價。」

Before and after each of the Fixings, there is an active principal trading market in loco London gold. Two-way buy-sell prices are quoted by market-makers in London and in major markets outside London. This system enables the continual trading of loco London gold round-the-clock on a worldwide basis. In view of this market development, the LBMA was incorporated in 1987 under the supervision of the Bank of England.

Bank of England in the City of London　位於倫敦中心的英倫銀行

每日倫敦議價的前後，本地倫敦金的買賣都十分活躍。市場莊家在倫敦及倫敦以外的主要市場定出雙向買賣價。這個制度使本地倫敦金市場能作二十四小時全球運作，亦由於市場的這個發展，倫敦金市協會便在英倫銀行的監督下，於1987年成立。

The unit of loco London gold trading is a bar weighing approximately 400 ounces troy conforming to Good Delivery Specifications. The gold content of each bar must be within 350 to 430 fine ounces and the weight must be expressed in ounces troy in multiples of 0.025 of an ounce. Each bar must be marked with a serial number, the fineness and the stamp of an acceptable melter and assayer (about 50 in the world).

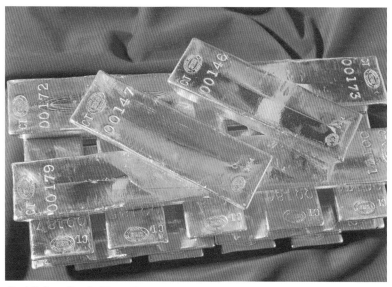

Good Delivery Standard Large Bars produced by Johnson Matthey, London
英國莊信萬豐鑄造符合國際規格的標準大條

本地倫敦金買賣單位是符合國際認許規格，重量約為400金衡盎司的金條，每條金條須含有350至430盎司的純金，而重量須為0.025盎司的倍數，並以金衡盎司為單位。每條金條刻有編號和成色與及認許熔鑄商及成色鑑定商（全世界約50家）的印鑑。

The minimum fineness is 995 parts per 1000 fine gold and gold said to be 1000 fine is marked down to 999.9 fine. The following fine gold contents of other bar weights are accepted by the LBMA. These bars are available at the spot loco London price plus a premium which varies dependent on prevailing market conditions in different locations.

Gross Weight 毛重	Fine Gold Contents in Ounces Troy 以金衡盎司計算的純金含量		
	Bars of 995.0 995.0成色條	Bars of 999.0 999.0成色條	Bars of 999.9 999.9成色條
1　Kilo 公斤	31.990	32.119	32.148
1/2 Kilo 公斤	15.995	16.059	16.074
100 Grams 克	3.199	3.212	3.215
50　Grams 克	1.600	1.607	1.608
10　Grams 克	0.321	0.322	0.322
5　Grams 克	0.161	0.161	0.161
10　Tolas 拖拉	3.731	3.746	3.750
5　Taels 両	5.987	6.011	6.017

Source　:　London Bullion Market Association, London
資料來源：　倫敦金市協會

黃金成色最少為千分之九百九十五，而稱為「千足純金」的金條，其標示純度則為999.9。以下為倫敦金市協會認可的其他重量的金條成色，這些金條通常以現貨本地倫敦金價加上按不同市場當時的狀況而變動的溢價進行買賣。

The loco London gold trading system was introduced to Hong Kong immediately after the gold market was liberalized in 1974. It is a spot market with the clearing of metal in London and payment of US dollars in New York two business days after the conclusion of a deal. Notwithstanding that the loco London gold market is a spot market, settlement can be deferred by making special credit facilities available to clients. These facilities normally involve the lending of gold and dollars, initial margins and variation margins, similar to the practice for gold futures trading. The

Gold Bars of 999.9 fine produced by Johnson Matthey, London
英國莊信萬豐鑄造的各種999.9純金條

於1974年黃金恢復在香港市場自由買賣後，本地倫敦金市場便開始在香港發展。這是一個現貨市場，黃金在倫敦交收，並在成交後的兩個交易日內在紐約以美元結算。儘管本地倫敦金市場是個現貨市場，客戶可利用特別的信貸安排而遞延

development of this mechanism led to the formation of a secondary deferred settlement market, as distinct from an inter-bank spot market, in which traders, manufacturers and producers in the world take part.

Should the price of gold advance to US$400 an ounce, for instance, the profit margin for some of the mining companies would be higher than the normal level. Under these circumstances, producers would be inclined to lock in the profit for a portion of their future mine production by selling a fixed amount of gold at the spot price.

A producer can, for example, sell 50,000 ounces of gold in the loco London gold deferred settlement market at US$400 an ounce to hedge against 20% of his production for the next 12 months. After the required facilities and

結算。這些安排一般牽涉借貸黃金或美元、基本保證金及價格變動保證金等,情況跟黃金期貨買賣相若。這個機制其後進一步發展,形成了一個本地倫敦金遞延結算市場。全球的黃金交易商、製造商及生產商均參與這個市場的買賣。

舉例來說,假如金價升至每盎司400美元,有些金礦公司的邊際利潤便會高出一般水平。在這個情況下,生產商會以現貨價沽出某數量的黃金,以保障他們未來礦產中部分的利潤。

例如生產商可在本地倫敦金遞延結算市場上以每盎司400美元的價格沽出50,000盎司黃金,為其在未來12個月的二成生產量作套戥。在與金業銀行辦妥必要的安排及文件後,銀行便將50,000盎司的黃金借予生產商,記入其黃金戶口。生產

documentation have been established with a bullion bank, the structure of the deal is that 50,000 ounces of gold would be leased to the producer and debited to his Metal Account. Gold interest at prevailing market rate would be debited to

The Hongkong and Shanghai Banking Corporation, Hong Kong　香港上海滙豐銀行

商須由交易日起支付按當時利率計算的黃金利息。同時，金業銀行以每盎司400美元代生產商沽售50,000盎司黃金，所

his Metal Account effective from the value date of the deal. Simultaneously, 50,000 ounces of gold would be sold on behalf of the producer at US$400 an ounce and the proceeds of US$20,000,000 and the interest at libid minus charges would be credited to his Dollar Account.

The producer can carry forward the deal until the quantity of gold is produced and delivered to the bank to unwind the deal. Alternatively, should the market price decline to a lower level, say US$370 an ounce, after conclusion of the deal and before delivery of the metal is effected, the producer can buy back from the bank 50,000 ounces of gold sold previously at US$400 an ounce to realise a profit of US$1,500,000 (50,000 x 30).

Under the market practice and depending on the credit standing of the producer, a fixed amount of initial margin has to be deposited with the bank to cover the deferred

得的20,000,000美元收益及按每日倫敦銀行同業拆息計算的利息，扣除有關費用後會存入生產商的美元戶口內。

生產商可無限期將交易遞延結算，直至該批黃金生產完成並交付銀行後，整項交易才告完結。但若黃金價格在交易未完成前下跌，例如滑落至每盎司370美元，生產商可向銀行購回其先前以每盎司400美元沽出的50,000盎司黃金而獲利1,500,000美元（50,000×30）。

按照市場的一般慣例，並視乎生產商的信用地位，生產商需在銀行存入一筆基本保證金以進行該宗遞延結算交易。此外，如金價升至高於其沽出價，生產商可能需繳付額外保證金（價格變動保證金），以保持原來基本保證金的水平。熱

settlement facility. Furthermore, should the market price move against the open position, the producer will be asked to make an extra deposit (variation margin) to maintain the original level of the initial margin. Similar types of deals can be undertaken by professional traders and individual speculators who are keen to take a view of the market.

When the price of gold dropped to US$372 an ounce on 3rd January 1995, a number of Asian traders and speculators bought the metal as they anticipated that the market would turn at this price level. The strong physical offtake in Asia at around US$370 an ounce experienced on previous occasions provided them with confidence. A trader could have bought, for example, 10,000 ounces loco London gold on 3rd January 1995 on deferred settlement basis and sold the same quantity when the price rose to US$388 an ounce on 10th March 1995. The accounting procedures would be as follows:

衷預測金價去向的專業買賣商及投機者均可進行類似的買賣。

1995年1月3日金價跌至每盎司372美元時，不少亞洲買賣商及投機者以遞延結算戶口購入黃金以建立好倉，他們預測金價跌至該水平將見底回升，因為過去數次當價格低見每盎司約370美元時，亞洲區實金購買量都大增，這種經驗，令投機者的信心加強。例如一名買賣商於1995年1月3日以遞延結算戶口買入10,000盎司本地倫敦金，並於1995年3月10日當金價升至每盎司388美元時沽出相同數量的黃金，買賣計算程序如下：

1. On 5th January 1995 (the value date of the buy order) the total value of the deal of US$3,720,000 (372 x 10,000) was debited to his Dollar Account.

2. Effective 5th January 1995, interest at Libor plus charges was debited to his Dollar Account daily.

3. On 14th March 1995 (the value date of the sell order), the total value of the deal of US$3,880,000 (388 x 10,000) was credited to his Dollar Account.

Assuming that the total interest covering the deferred settlement period amounted to US$40,000, the realized profit for the deal would be US$120,000 being the dealing profit of US$160,000 (3,880,000 - 3,720,000) minus the interest charge incurred.

1. 於1995年1月5日（買入結算日）在其美元戶口記借買賣總額共3,720,000美元（372×10,000）。

2. 由1995年1月5日起，以倫敦銀行同業拆息計算的利息連費用每日從其美元戶口扣除。

3. 於1995年3月14日（沽出結算日）將買賣總額共3,880,000美元（388×10,000）存入其美元戶口。

假設有關遞延結算期間所須支付的利息總額為40,000美元，從該項買賣獲得的利潤為120,000美元，即買賣利潤160,000美元（3,880,000－3,720,000）減去利息後的數額。

On the other hand, the trader would lose money if the price of gold declined after 3rd January 1995. Furthermore, should the initial margin drop below the original level due to adverse price movements, variation margin would be called. If the respective amount was not deposited, the outstanding position would be closed and any loss incurred would be carried by the trader. These conditions are stipulated in the agreement which the customer would be asked to sign before any trading would commence.

The loco London gold market runs in parallel to the Exchange and in view of the different trading unit, price denomination, fineness of tael gold bars and interest payment system, arbitrage opportunities are available at times. The position can be set up by buying loco London gold and selling simultaneously an equivalent amount of tael gold in the Exchange (bear arbitrage) or vice versa (bull arbitrage). Given below is the formula to calculate the

另一方面，倘1995年1月3日後金價下跌，該買賣商便會蒙受虧損。此外，當由於金價走勢與預期相反，致令原有的基本保證金不足時，便需補交價格變動保證金。如未能及時存入該等保證金，則其持有的好倉或淡倉，將以市價沽出或買入，有關的虧損由該買賣商承擔。此等條件均列入合約內，客戶須簽署合約後方能進行買賣。

實際上，本地倫敦金市場與貿易場並行營運，但由於彼此所用的交易單位、定價貨幣、金條成色及利息支付制度各異，因此套戥機會時有出現。在這種情況下，可買入本地倫敦金而同時在貿易場沽出等值數量的両金（賣空套戥）或作相反

premium of tael gold over the level of loco London gold price:

Assumption :

Tael Gold Price   :   HK\$3,495 per tael
Loco London Gold Price   :   US\$378 per troy oz
US\$/HK\$ TT   :   US\$1 = HK\$7.7250

$$\text{Tael Premium} = (3{,}495 \div 1.20337 \div 0.99 \div 7.7250) - 378$$
$$= 379.80 - 378.00$$
$$= \text{US\$1.80 per troy ounce}$$

The normal practice is to undertake deals for 1,700 taels against 2,000 troy ounces each. Under the above assumptions, the unrealized book profit for setting up the bear arbitrage by selling tael gold (1,700 taels @HK\$3,495) and buying loco London gold (2,000 ounces @US\$378) is US\$3,600

買賣（買空套戥），以開立套戥倉（開倉）。以下是計算價格升水的公式：

假設：

貿易場金價   : 每兩3,495港元
本地倫敦金價   : 每金衡盎司378美元
美元/港元電滙價   : 1美元＝7.7250港元

$$兩升水 = (3{,}495 \div 1.20337 \div 0.99 \div 7.7250) - 378$$
$$= 379.80 - 378.00$$
$$= 1.80美元（每金衡盎司）$$

一般的做法是以1,700兩與2,000金衡盎司作套戥；按照上述的假設，沽出1,700兩兩金（每兩3,495港元）及買入2,000盎

(2,000 x 1.80). At this point, there is an open foreign exchange position which should be covered. The total value of US$756,000 (2,000 x 378) covering the deal should be bought for payment to the gold seller. The HK$ equivalent value of HK$5,840,100 (756,000 x 7.7250) can be borrowed from the Bank.

Bank for International Settlements, Basle　巴塞爾國際結算銀行

司本地倫敦金（每盎司378美元），在賣空套戥上所得的未實現賬面利潤為3,600美元（2,000×1.80）。為清除買入本地倫敦金所欠美元的外滙風險，應買入756,000美元（2,000×378）付給賣家。該相當於5,840,100港元（756,000×7.7250）的數額可向銀行借貸。

Having concluded the first part of the arbitrage deal as described above, the remaining variables are spot tael gold prices (at premium or discount to loco London gold), carried over charges (contango or backwardation) and money cost (HK$ overnight lending or borrowing rates). The following are the factors which determine the actual profit or loss.

Firstly, tael gold should normally be traded at a premium above loco London gold and the amount should be equivalent to the freight, insurance and manufacturing charges (CIF premium) for delivering tael bars to the Exchange. However, the premium fluctuates largely in accordance with the open interest of the Exchange and prevailing sentiment of the investors. On certain occasions, tael gold is traded at discount to loco London gold.

In the case of the example given earlier, should the premium of US$1.80 decline to US$0.50 an ounce, for instance, the

如上所述開立套戥倉後，其他變數為現貨兩金價（相對於本地倫敦金是高水或低水）、議定倉費（高息或低息）及港元貸款成本（港元隔夜借貸利率）。以下是決定套戥倉的實際利潤或虧損的因素。

首先，兩金通常以高於本地倫敦金的價格買賣，而高水的數額應相等於將兩條交付貿易場的到岸價溢價。然而，視乎當時投機者對市場走勢的推測及未平倉的數量，兩價高低水每日浮動。在某些情況下，兩金買賣價比對本地倫敦金會呈現低水。

在上述例子中，如每盎司1.80美元的高水在套戥後下降至0.50美元，套戥者可平倉套利，買入1,700兩兩金而沽出

arbitrageur can take advantage of the situation and reverse the deal. This means that he would buy back 1,700 taels of tael gold and sell 2,000 ounces of loco London gold to realize a total profit of US$2,600 (2,000 x 1.80 – 2,000 x 0.5) plus or minus interest charges.

Should the premium continue to advance and exceed US$1.80 per ounce, the arbitrageur can take delivery of the

Swiss Bank Corporation, Zurich   蘇黎世瑞士銀行

2,000盎司本地倫敦金，未計利息收支前獲取2,600美元（2,000×1.80－2,000×0.50）的利潤。

如高水持續升至每盎司1.80美元以上，套戥者可收取買入的2,000盎司本地倫敦金標準大條，然後化為両條。化工費用一般約在每盎司1.00美元至1.50美元之間，視乎當時両條的

2,000 ounces of loco London gold purchased and make arrangement for the large standard bars to be transformed into tael bars. The transformation charge fluctuates normally between US$1.00 to US$1.50 per ounce dependent on the prevailing supply and demand. The tael bars can then be delivered to the Exchange to unwind the arbitrage with a profit of US$0.30 to US$0.80 per ounce. The essence of the operation is to avoid building up a bear arbitrage position when the tael premium is below the transformation charge.

On the other hand, bull arbitrage deals can be undertaken on the same principle when tael gold is available at discount to loco London gold. Should the discount exceed the CIF premium substantially, tael bars can be bought and converted into Good Delivery standard large bars for delivery to the London Gold Market to unwind the deal.

Secondly, the Carried Over Charge (COC) rate should normally be negative (i.e. sellers receive COC from those

供求情況而定。製成的兩條可交付貿易場抵沖套戥倉,而賺取每盎司0.30美元至0.80美元的利潤。從高水或低水的角度,套戥運作的要點是避免在兩金的高水低於化工費用情況下,開立賣空套戥倉。

同樣的道理亦適用於在兩金價格低於本地倫敦金價下的買空套戥。如低水大大超逾到岸價溢價,則可買入兩條,將之化為國際認許標準大條,交付倫敦黃金市場以抵沖套戥倉。

其次,議定倉費通常應該是低息(即是沒有足夠資金收取實金的買家付出議定倉費),而倉費應相當於港元隔夜貸款利

buyers who do not have sufficient funds to pay for the purchase) and should be equivalent to the overnight cost of HK$. However, the contango and backwardation rates exceed the normal limit sometimes and adversely affect the profit of the arbitrage. Should this be the case, delivery of the tael bars sold should be effected to unwind the deal.

Deutsche Bank AG, Frankfurt　　德國德意志銀行，法蘭克福

息。不過倉費有時會出現超出一般水平的高息或低息，影響套戥的利潤，在此情況下，可進行兩條交付安排，抵冲套戥倉。

Thirdly, when there is a shortage of tael bars, positive COC rate (contango) would apply. This means that the bull arbitrageur receives interest on the HK$ deposit plus the COC covering the long position in the Exchange. On the other hand, the bear arbitrageur has to pay both the interest for the borrowing of HK$ and the COC for the short position of tael gold. Under these circumstances, the bear arbitrageur should arrange for the delivery of tael bars to the Exchange to unwind the deal.

Another type of facility available in the loco London market is the gold loan. The tenor of the loan varies depending on individual requirements of the borrowers. Interest charge is based on the spot gold market value and the prevailing gold interest rate on the drawdown date. This facility is widely utilized by local jewellery manufacturers in Hong Kong as a hedging and financing instrument.

第三，當両條供應短缺，議定倉費便會出現高息（順價）的情況，這時買空套戥者除收取港元存款的利息外，還可收取在貿易場買空的議定倉費，而賣空套戥者則要支付港元借款的利息及賣空両金的議定倉費。在此等情況下，賣空套戥者應安排將両條交付貿易場以抵冲套戥倉。

在本地倫敦金市場可採用的另一種信貸方式是借金。借金的期限視乎借方個別需要而定，利息按交收日期的金價與現貨黃金息率計算。這種信貸方式為香港金飾製造商普遍採用作對冲及融資工具。

For example, a manufacturer is required to keep constantly 1,000 ounces of finished articles in stocks for sale to his customers. Subject to satisfactory negotiation, he can make an arrangement with a bullion bank to borrow 1,000 ounces of gold monthly for this purpose. Assuming that the spot gold price is US$385 an ounce and the gold interest rate is 3.50% per annum, the interest calculation is illustrated below:

Tenor   :   1 month (30 days)
Quantity   :   1,000 troy ounces
Spot Gold Interest :   3.5% per annum
Spot Gold Price   :   US$385 per troy ounce

$$\text{Loan Interest} = \frac{1,000 \text{ x } 385 \text{ x } 0.035 \text{ x } 30}{360}$$

$$= \text{US\$1,122.90}$$

例如，製造商需要長期儲備1,000盎司黃金製品存貨以售予顧客，可與金業銀行洽商，安排每月借入1,000盎司黃金。假設現貨金價是每盎司385美元，年息率為3.50%，借入1,000盎司黃金須付利息計算如下：

借金期限   :   1個月（30日）
數量   :   1,000金衡盎司
現貨黃金息率   :   每年3.5%
現貨金價   :   每金衡盎司385美元

$$\text{借金利息} = \frac{1,000 \times 385 \times 0.035 \times 30}{360}$$

$$= 1,122.90\text{美元}$$

The total interest charge of US$1,122.90 is payable on the maturity date of the loan when the full quantity of the gold is returned to the lender. The loan can also be rolled over for another period subject to the negotiation between the lender and borrower.

South African Reserve Bank, Pretoria
南非儲備銀行，比勒陀利亞

金飾製造商於到期日須支付的利息總額為1,122.90美元，屆時並須歸還所借全數黃金。經借貸雙方協商同意，亦可延續借金的期限。

Credit terms governing gold borrowing facilities are comparable with those covering bank loans. Normally, securities in various acceptable forms are pledged to the lender if cash payment of the initial margin is not made by the borrower.

The worldwide contraction of the bullion industry in the past 10 years has greatly reduced the number of participants in the market. Currently, the active foreign institutions engaged in loco London gold trading in Hong Kong include AIG, Barclays Bank, Credit Suisse, Deutsche Bank, Republic National Bank of New York, Smith Barney, Standard Chartered Bank – The Mocatta Group, Standard Bank of London, Rothschild, Swiss Bank Corporation and Union Bank of Switzerland. The volume of business has also declined and existing turnover is in the region of 1,000,000 ounces daily.

借金的信貸條款與向銀行借款類同。一般來說，如借金者並非以現金支付基本保證金，則須以各種可接受的抵押品作押。

由於全球金業在過去十年呈現收縮，金商的數目因而大大減少。以下是目前在香港積極參與本地倫敦金買賣的外國金商：美國國際集團、巴克萊銀行、瑞士信貸銀行、德意志銀行、美國利寶銀行、美邦金融、標準渣打銀行 － 慕加達、英國標旗銀行、羅富齊、瑞士銀行及瑞士聯合銀行。黃金買賣活動亦同時下降，現時每日交投量約為1,000,000盎司。

THE PHYSICAL GOLD MARKET

實 金 市 場

Chinese people are great lovers for gold or "kam" as it is called in Chinese. Articles produced with the yellow metal ranging from rings to watches and earrings to bracelets are worn by Chinese as a symbol of wealth and kept as stored value. In the old days, false teeth were made of gold and this remains the practice among some of the older people in China, Taiwan and Hong Kong. For affluent Chinese families, gold figurines representing fortune, prosperity and longevity as well as gold figures of Buddha are displayed in their homes. On auspicious occasions such as the New Year in the Chinese lunar calendar, gold-related phrases are used to express our good wishes. "Kam Ngan Moon Uk" and "Kam Yuk Moon Tong" are commonly used to indicate the wish that our houses would be full of gold and silver or gold and jade.

Gold has also long been considered by the Chinese as a hard currency. With the constant changing of power of the many emperors, dynasties and ruling parties in China, the metal

中國人熱愛黃金，喜愛配戴「金器」，包括金戒指、手錶、耳環以及手鐲等，以象徵財富及作保值用途。昔日曾經流行用黃金製造假牙，現時中國、台灣及香港一些老一輩的人仍有鑲配金牙。在一些富裕的中國家庭，家裏亦愛放置黃金擺件，例如「福、祿、壽」的金像以及金佛。在傳統節日如農曆新年，也會以黃金有關的吉祥語句互相祝賀，例如「金銀滿屋」及「金玉滿堂」便一般用來祝福家裏滿載黃金和白銀或黃金和翠玉。

一直以來，中國人視黃金為一種流通貨幣，而在中國歷史上每當改朝換代，或政治動盪期間，人們都會購買及收藏黃金，作為抗衡政治動盪的保障及自身的保險。

has been bought and hoarded as a hedge against political uncertainties and as a kind of life insurance.

Tael bars with a fineness of 990 produced by acceptable melters of the Chinese Gold & Silver Exchange remain the most popular item among consumers. These bars are bought and sold over the counters of hundreds of local banks, jewellery shops and money changers. Bid and offer prices follow closely the spot prices quoted in the Exchange and bars of 999.9 fine in various sizes are also available at a premium.

Tael Bars produced by Lee Cheong Gold Dealer　利昌金鋪鑄造的兩條

由金銀業貿易場認許的熔鑄商所生產的990成色金條易於銷售，一直甚受香港人歡迎。這些兩條在香港各大銀行、金飾行及找換店均可買賣，買賣價與貿易場的現貨價相差甚少。不同大小的999.9成色金條亦可加付溢價購買。

Tael Bars produced by King Fook Gold & Jewellery Co., Limited 景福珠寶鐘錶公司鑄造的両條

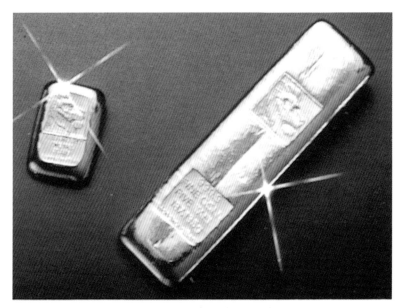

Tael Bars produced by HongkongBank　滙豐銀行鑄造的両條

The liberalization of gold trading in Hong Kong in 1974 added a new dimension to the local physical market. Good Delivery bars were imported from London and Switzerland and gained gradual acceptability in Hong Kong. In the early stage of development, prices were based on spot loco London quotations plus a CIF premium which varies according to sizes and purities of the bars. The price structure has now changed and these imported bars are sold in Hong Kong at tael gold prices quoted in the Exchange plus a swap premium. Assuming that the spot price quoted in the Exchange is HK$3,495 per tael and that the swap premium is HK$40 per tael, the following formula illustrates the price calculation for 1 kilobar of 999.9 fine:

$$\text{Price (1 kilobar)} = \frac{(3,495 + 40) \times 32.1507 \times 0.9999}{1.20337}$$

$$= \text{HK\$94,435.90}$$

黃金於1974年恢復在香港自由買賣後，本地實金市場即進入一個新天地。由倫敦及瑞士進口的國際認許金條漸受香港人歡迎。初時，價格是以本地倫敦金現貨價加到岸價溢價為準，而到岸價溢價則按金條的大小及純度而定。現時價格結構已有改變，這些進口金條以貿易場所定的兩價加對換溢價買賣。假設貿易場所定的現貨價為每兩3,495港元，對換溢價為每兩40港元，以下是一公斤999.9純度國際認許金條價格的計算公式：

$$\text{價格（1公斤裝金條）} = \frac{(3,495 + 40) \times 32.1507 \times 0.9999}{1.20337}$$

$$= 94,435.90\text{港元}$$

Fine Gold Bars produced by Hang Seng Bank　　恒生銀行鑄造的足金金條

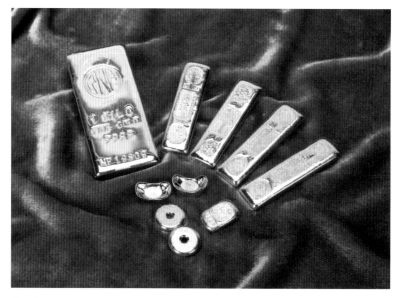

Tael Gold Bars produced by Hing Fung Goldsmith & Refinery Limited
慶豐金鋪鑄造的両條

Additional to the acceptable melters of the Chinese Gold & Silver Exchange, Johnson Matthey, Métaux Précieux S.A. Metalor and Hereaus are also engaged in the precious metal refining business in Hong Kong. They have established refineries in the territory and produce gold bars of 9999 fine, gold chemicals and other precious metal products to cater for the requirements of the local jewellery, electronic and the electroplating industries.

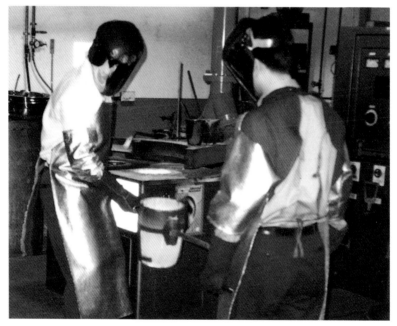

The Gold Refinery of Johnson Matthey Hong Kong Limited　　香港莊信萬豐的鑄金工場

除金銀業貿易場認許的熔鑄商外，莊信萬豐、瑞士金銀及賀利氏亦有在香港經營貴金屬精煉業務，在香港設立鑄造工場，生產9999成色金條、黃金化工原料及其他貴金屬製品，供應香港的首飾製造商、電子及電鍍業之用。

The steady economic growth in Hong Kong since the mid 1980s has greatly increased the income of the people and this has in turn stimulated a higher level of gold offtake. The per capita consumption of 7.66 grammes in 1994 was the second highest in the Asia-Pacific region. The table appended below provides the estimated offtake by the largest consuming countries in Asia.

由於香港經濟自八零年代中起穩步增長，港人入息大幅提升，因而增加黃金的銷售量。香港在1994年的人均黃金購買量估計為7.66克，是亞太區第二位。下表是各亞洲國家的估計實金購買量。

Country 國家	Population 人口	Per Capita GDP 1994 1994年人均國內生產總值	1994 Gold Consumption 1994年黃金購買量	
			Total 總量	Per Capita 人均量
	'000 千人	US$ 美元	Kilos 公斤	Grammes 克
India 印度	918,200	1,250	415,000	0.45
Japan 日本	125,400	21,090	229,000	1.83
China 中國	1,202,900	2,428	224,000	0.19
Taiwan 台灣	21,300	12,315	162,000	7.60
Thailand 泰國	60,400	6,390	124,000	2.05
S. Korea 南韓	44,900	9,810	106,000	2.36
Indonesia 印尼	194,700	3,140	97,000	0.50
Hong Kong 香港	6,200	21,670	47,500	7.66
Vietnam 越南	74,000	1,263	28,000	0.38
Malaysia 馬來西亞	19,600	8,630	25,000	1.28
Singapore 新加坡	3,100	20,470	24,000	7.74
Myanmar 緬甸	46,000	676	17,000	0.37

Sources : Asiaweek, World Gold Council, Standard London (Asia) Limited
資料來源： 亞洲週刊、世界黃金協會、英國標旗（亞洲）有限公司

Additional to gold bars of various sizes and purities, international bullion coins and medals are also marketed extensively in Hong Kong. These include the Canadian Maple Leaf, American Eagle, Australian Nugget, British Britannia, Chinese Panda and South African Krugerrand. The selling premium of these coins fluctuates marginally at around 3.75% over the intrinsic value of gold and sales have been relatively steady. The importation of gold coins into Hong Kong from various countries during the past five years is summarized in the table appended below:

除不同重量和純度的金條外，國際金幣如加拿大楓葉、美國鷹揚、澳洲鴻運、英國皇家、中國熊貓及南非富格林等在香港亦廣受歡迎。這些金幣售價通常較金磚價值高出約3.75%，銷路都很穩定，過去五年從各國進口香港金幣數字摘錄如下：

Kilos 公斤

Country 國家	1990	1991	1992	1993	1994
Australia 澳洲	1,436	984	2,167	2,057	3,637
Canada 加拿大	3,940	1,139	2,247	962	516
China 中國	1,138	1,160	381	469	456
Germany Fed Rep 德國	1	311	127	827	–
Switzerland 瑞士	221	439	292	–	69
United Kingdom 英國	528	36	29	804	–
Others 其他	405	722	37	157	325
Total 總數	7,669	4,791	5,280	5,276	5,003

Source : Census and Statistics Department, Hong Kong Government
資料來源： 香港政府統計處

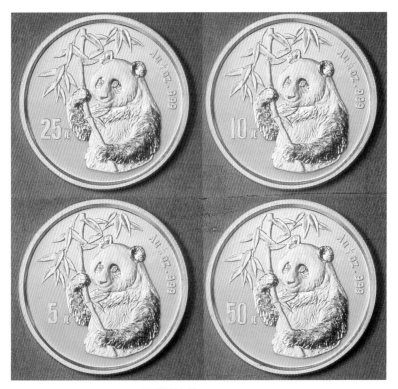

Chinese Panda Gold Coins   中國熊貓金幣

Canadian Maple Leaf Gold Coins   加拿大楓葉金幣

American Eagle Gold Coin　　美國鷹揚金幣

Australian Nugget Gold Coins　　澳洲鴻運金幣

British Britannia Gold Coin　　英國皇家金幣

South African Krugerrand Gold Coins　　南非富格林金幣

The South African Krugerrand gold coin was the first bullion coin introduced to Hong Kong by International Gold Corporation, Johannesburg, in the early 1970s. Subsequently, other bullion coins were imported and sold in the territory. Hong Kong issued the first gold coin in 1975 to commemorate the first visit of Her Majesty the Queen and His Royal Highness The Prince Philip, Duke of Edinburgh, to the colony. Gold coins with a face value of HK$1,000 were made legal tender for the payment of any amount with effect from 5th May 1975. The coins are in 22 carat gold and are

The Commemorative Gold Coin issued by Hong Kong Government in 1975
1975年香港政府發行的紀念金幣

南非富格林金幣是最早引進香港的外國金幣，由約翰內斯堡國際黃金公司於1970年代初在香港推出，之後其他金幣相繼輸入香港發售。香港於1975年發行首枚金幣以紀念英女皇及愛丁堡公爵菲臘親王伉儷首次訪港。金幣面值1,000港元，

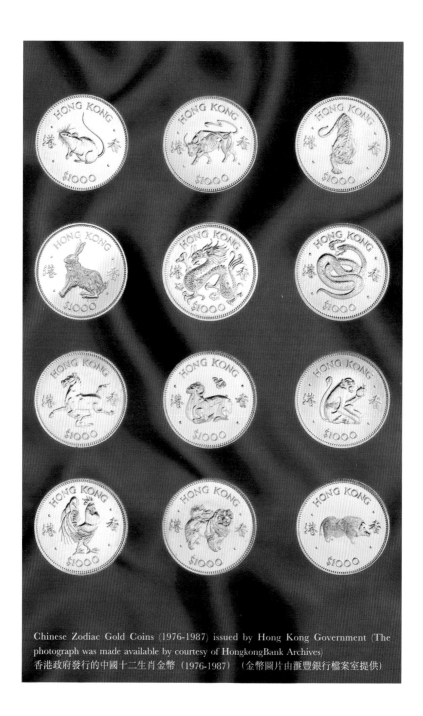

Chinese Zodiac Gold Coins (1976-1987) issued by Hong Kong Government (The photograph was made available by courtesy of HongkongBank Archives)
香港政府發行的中國十二生肖金幣（1976-1987）（金幣圖片由滙豐銀行檔案室提供）

available in both proof and uncirculated versions. Each coin measures 28.4 mm in diameter and weights 15.976 grammes.

Other gold coins with identical specifications subsequently issued are related to the legendary animals of the Chinese lunar calendar. One of the most important festivals in the lunar calendar is the New Year which begins on the first day of the first lunar month. The years are represented by 12 animal symbols that are repeated in a cycle. The animals of the 12-year cycle are the rat, ox, tiger, rabbit, dragon, snake, horse, goat, monkey, cockerel, dog and pig. The first day of the lunar year falls either in January or February.

According to the legend, people born in the Year of the Rat, for instance, are generally optimistic, sociable and sentimental. Rat persons adapt easily to a new environment and have critical minds and rich imagination.

由1975年5月5日起可作為合法貨幣使用。金幣以22K金鑄造，備有標準及珍藏裝，每枚金幣直徑28.4毫米，重15.976克。

隨後發行規格相同的金幣，是與中國農曆年傳統的十二生肖有關。農曆新年是中國人最重要的節日之一，新年由農曆正月第一日開始計算。中國人以不同動物代表十二個年份，作為一個循環，稱為十二生肖，其順序為鼠、牛、虎、兔、龍、蛇、馬、羊、猴、雞、狗、豬。農曆年初一通常在西曆一月或二月之間。

根據傳說，不同生肖的人有不同的性格，例如鼠年出生的人一般都較樂觀、合群和感性。屬鼠的人容易適應新環境、具有批判能力和豐富的想像力。

The issue of the coins in a series to mark the 12 lunar years fell in the western calendar years 1976-1987. The obverse of each coin bears the symbol of one of the 12 animals and the reverse displays the portrait of Her Majesty The Queen.

To commemorate the second visit (1986) to Hong Kong of Her Majesty Queen Elizabeth II and His Royal Highness The Prince Philip, Duke of Edinburgh, the Government issued a gold coin bearing the new Raphael Maklouf portrait of Her Majesty The Queen.

The Commemorative Gold Coin issued by Hong Kong Government in 1986
1986年香港政府發行的紀念金幣

1976-1987年間香港政府發行一系列十二生肖紀念金幣，每個金幣正面為十二生肖裏代表某一個生肖的標記，背面則刻有英女皇的肖像。

為紀念英女皇伊利沙白二世與愛丁堡公爵菲臘親王1986年第二次訪港，港府發行了刻有由拉菲爾麥洛夫繪畫的英女皇全新肖像金幣。

The 1975 and 1986 Royal visit coins and the series of coins to mark the twelve lunar years were the only legal tender gold coins issued by the Hong Kong Government. This set of fourteen coins will become unique in the history of Hong Kong when the sovereignty is returned to China in 1997.

Aside from selling gold coins, a number of local banks in Hong Kong offer their customers facilities for investing in gold. The Hongkong and Shanghai Banking Corporation (HongkongBank), for example, offers three different ways for their clients to invest in their "Wayfoong Gold" which include "Wayfoong Passbook Gold", "Wayfoong Statement Gold" and "Wayfoong Gold Bars". Details of the transactions are highlighted by HongkongBank as follows:

–　　Wayfoong Passbook Gold and Wayfoong Statement Gold are not required to be backed up by physical gold. All transactions made also do not involve any physical gold.

1975年及1986年的女皇訪港金幣及十二生肖紀念金幣是唯一兩種由香港政府發行可作為合法貨幣使用的金幣。這套十四枚紀念金幣在1997年香港主權移交中國後將成為香港歷史上的陳蹟。

除售賣金幣外，不少香港本地銀行均有為客戶提供投資黃金的服務。例如香港上海滙豐銀行（滙豐銀行）便為客戶提供三種不同方式以投資其「滙豐金」，包括「滙豐金存摺」、「滙豐黃金券」及「滙豐千足黃金」。滙豐銀行提供的買賣詳情概述如下：

—　　滙豐金存摺及滙豐黃金券均毋須以實金交收，所有買賣完全不牽涉任何實金。

Wayfoong Gold Passbook of The Hongkong and Shanghai Banking Corporation
香港上海滙豐銀行的滙豐金存摺

Notional Precious Metals Passbook of Po Sang Bank Ltd.　寶生銀行的「金銀寶」存摺

- There are absolutely no charges other than the actual buying or selling price at the time of transaction.

- HongkongBank guarantees to buy back any amount of Wayfoong Gold at the current quoted price (provided the Wayfoong Gold Bars are not damaged).

- Wayfoong Gold Bars cannot be directly transferred to Wayfoong Passbook Gold or Wayfoong Statement Gold.

- Whether the customers choose to invest in Wayfoong Passbook Gold, Wayfoong Statement Gold or Wayfoong Gold Bars, they can carry out transactions either by cash, cashier's order or by Current or Savings account transfer.

- Wayfoong Passbook Gold and Wayfoong Statement Gold Holdings may be used as collateral for a Current Account overdraft.

— 除買賣時的實際買入價或賣出價外，完全不收取任何費用。

— 滙豐銀行保證以當時牌價購回任何數額的滙豐金（惟滙豐千足黃金須完整而並無損毀）。

— 滙豐千足黃金不能直接轉撥往滙豐金存摺或滙豐黃金券戶口。

— 不論客戶選擇投資滙豐金存摺、滙豐黃金券或滙豐千足黃金，均可以現金、銀行本票或由來往戶口或儲蓄戶口轉賬以進行買賣。

— 持有滙豐金存摺及滙豐黃金券可用作來往戶口的透支抵押。

All gold transactions are recorded in a special Gold Passbook and each transaction entry gives details of quantity, date and market price. There is no risk of loss through theft or misplacement of passbook. Overall, it is a convenient way to invest in gold without any security or storage problem.

The parent company of HongkongBank, HSBC Holdings Plc, also owns Midland Bank PLC, one of the five fixing members of the London Bullion Market Association. In this capacity, they are actively engaged in loco London gold trading in the world market.

Po Sang Bank and other members of the Bank of China Group, Standard Chartered Bank, Hang Seng Bank and Wing Hang Bank offer similar types of passbook gold trading facilities to their clients.

Hong Kong does not have any gold mine production. Gold required for industrial and other uses is imported directly

所有黃金買賣均在一本特別的黃金存摺內記錄，列明每一次買賣的數量、日期及市價等資料，客戶不會因存摺被竊或遺失而招致損失。整體來說，這種投資黃金的方法非常方便，可免除保安或收藏的問題。

滙豐銀行的母公司，滙豐控股有限公司亦擁有倫敦金市協會五名議價金商之一的米特蘭銀行，因此間接在世界本地倫敦金市場亦十分活躍。

寶生銀行及其他中國銀行集團的成員、渣打銀行、恒生銀行及永亨銀行亦有為客戶提供類似的存摺黃金買賣服務。

from producing countries in the world or from other trading centres. The metal is shipped to Hong Kong in various forms and purities to suit different applications. For jewellery manufacture and gold refining, large standard bars and kilobars of 995.0/999.9 fine are normally imported. For the electroplating and electronic industry, gold is consumed in fabricated or semi-fabricated forms including gold alloys, gold wires and chemical gold products. Dores and scraps with lower gold contents are also imported by local refiners in Hong Kong, particularly from neighbouring countries in the region.

In 1994, Hong Kong imported officially 326.10 tonnes of gold with a total value of HK$31,200 million (US$4,050 million). The major sources of supplies are North America, South Africa, Switzerland, United Kingdom, Australia and Canada.

香港並沒有任何金礦，工業及其他用途的黃金均直接由世界各地的產金國家及其他黃金市場進口。輸入香港的黃金的形狀及純度不一，以適合不同的用途。製造珠寶首飾及冶金一般進口995.0/999.9成色的標準大條及公斤條；電鍍及電子業方面則購入黃金製成品及半製成品，包括K金片、金線及黃金化工原料。在香港的本地煉金商亦會自鄰近國家輸入含金量較低的金屑。

1994年，香港共進口黃金326.10公噸，總值312億港元（40.50億美元）。主要黃金供應國家為北美洲、南非、瑞士、英國、澳洲及加拿大。

Gold Bars imported into Hong Kong from Switzerland
從瑞士進口香港的各種金條

During the past five years, Hong Kong imported a total of 1,364 tonnes of gold in different forms and purities from various countries. Judging from past experience, standard large bars of 999.9 fine are supplied by North America while kilobars of 999.9 fine are shipped from South Africa, Europe and Australia. Breakdown statistics covering the importation of gold bullion into Hong Kong during the period of 1990-1994 are summarised in the table appended below:

過去五年，香港從其他國家進口不同形狀及純度的黃金共1,364公噸。根據以往的經驗，999.9成色標準大條一般來自北美洲；而999.9成色公斤條則主要來自南非、歐洲及澳洲。1990-1994年間香港的黃金進口統計數字節錄如下：

Tonnes 公噸

Country 國家	1990	1991	1992	1993	1994
U.S.A. 美國	39.80	83.80	56.50	32.10	76.40
South Africa 南非	0.80	20.60	41.50	57.60	67.00
Switzerland 瑞士	74.00	77.60	84.30	49.90	62.00
United Kingdom 英國	24.70	20.20	44.50	22.30	36.30
Australia 澳洲	15.40	35.80	38.60	38.70	24.00
Canada 加拿大	14.70	30.00	30.20	5.60	23.60
Philippines 菲律賓	2.70	8.90	23.50	6.10	–
Others 其他	5.00	18.60	15.70	18.20	36.80
Total 總數	177.10	295.50	334.80	230.50	326.10

Source   :   Census and Statistics Department, Hong Kong Government
資料來源 ： 香港政府統計處

On the export side, Hong Kong was the leading physical gold distribution centre in Asia while the Hongkong-Macau gold trade lasted. This special role played by Hong Kong has gradually diminished since the mid 1970s following the liberalization of gold markets in neighbouring countries. However, the unofficial export trade has been re-established as a result of higher Chinese demand since the mid 1980s. Hong Kong, being the gateway to China, has become the leading supplier of gold in various forms to people living in the Mainland.

Over the last few years, traditional gold hoarders in Hong Kong and in other countries in Southeast Asia have become more price sensitive and they tend to take advantage of the short-term price volatility and trend. On the run up in the price to US$400 an ounce in May 1995, liquidation by Asian physical gold hoarders was experienced and this practice is expected to prevail until a long-term rising price trend develops.

出口方面，在香港－澳門黃金貿易蓬勃期間，香港曾是亞洲的實金分銷中心，但自七零年代中起，由於鄰近國家逐漸開放黃金市場，香港這個特殊地位便日趨沒落。然而，由於中國大陸經濟自八零年代中急劇增長，對黃金的需求大增。香港位處中國的南大門，供應中國大陸人民的黃金及各種金飾漸增，使香港非正式黃金出口業務再度蓬勃起來。

在過往數年，香港及東南亞其他地區的黃金長線投資者越加留意金價動向，並利用黃金的短期價格波動及走勢賺取利潤。在1995年5月金價升至每盎司400美元期間，很多亞洲人都將所持有的實金變現，預期這種現象仍會持續，直至長期金價升勢確立為止。

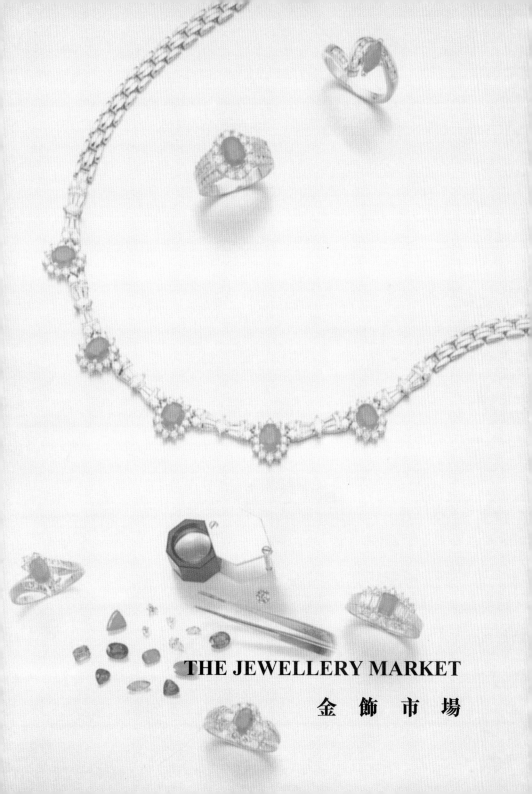

THE JEWELLERY MARKET

金 飾 市 場

The jewellery market in Hong Kong has been developing from strength to strength. There are more than 1,800 jewellery retail shops and 1,100 manufacturers engaged in the industry which fabricated 91 tonnes of fine gold in 1994. Aside from the higher domestic demand, the booming tourist industry and the increased export trade have contributed significantly to the growth.

Hong Kong is the world's third largest exporter of carat jewellery after Italy and Switzerland. The industry focuses more on fine jewellery incorporating precious and semi-precious stones, set in yellow and white carat gold and platinum. Diamonds, rubies, sapphires, emeralds, jade, cultured pearls and opals are very much in demand, although point-size diamonds remain the most popular items. These stones are imported into Hong Kong from various countries including South Africa, Belgium, Myanmar, Thailand, Russia, Sri Lanka, and China.

香港的金飾市場一直有良好的發展。全港現有珠寶首飾店超過1,800家，製造商1,100多家，在1994年製成品約為純金91公噸。除本地有強大的需求外，蓬勃的旅遊業及出口貿易增長亦大大促進了這個市場的發展。

香港是世界第三大K金首飾出口商，僅次於意大利及瑞士。珠寶首飾業的發展主要集中於精純首飾，即是以寶石或半寶石鑲嵌於K金或白金上的首飾。市場對鑽石、紅寶石、藍寶石、綠寶石、翡翠、養珠、蛋白石等都需求甚殷，這些寶石由南非、比利時、緬甸、泰國、俄羅斯、斯里蘭卡及中國各地進口香港，其中以碎鑽最受歡迎。

The Most Popular Precious Stones in Hong Kong (Articles produced by Continental Jewellery (Mfg.) Limited) 香港最流行的寶石（恒和珠寶首飾廠的製品）

With the high quality of craftsmanship and innovative contemporary designs, manufacturers in Hong Kong are well placed to produce different types of jewellery articles to suit individual taste and affordability. The products have broadened greatly in recent years, ranging from high fashion carat jewellery to chuk kam (pure gold) adornments and figurines. Gem-set jewellery articles in the medium price range are the best selling items which include rings, earrings, necklaces, bracelets, pendants, brooches and cuff-links.

香港製造商憑藉高超的手工及新穎趨時的設計，已能緊隨顧客的個人品味及購買能力而製造不同種類的珠寶首飾。近年，金飾的種類不斷擴展，由時尚K金飾以至足金首飾、小巧配飾及各種擺件。中價的鑲石首飾的銷路最佳，包括戒指、耳環、項鍊、手鐲、吊咀、胸針及袖口鈕等。

Carat Jade Jewellery produced by King Fook Gold & Jewellery Co., Limited
景福珠寶鐘錶公司生產的翠玉首飾

Carat Pearl Jewellery produced by King Fook Gold & Jewellery Co., Limited
景福珠寶鐘錶公司生產的珍珠首飾

Carat Jewellery produced by Chow Tai Fook Jewellery Co., Limited
周大福珠寶金行生產的K金首飾

Carat Jewellery produced by Tse Sui Luen Jewellery Co., Limited
謝瑞麟珠寶有限公司生產的K金首飾

Carat Jewellery produced by Larry Jewellery Co., Limited
俊文寶石店生產的K金首飾

The gold watches....
at the end of the rainbow

Jewellery Watch produced by Myer Jewelry Mfr. Limited
萬雅珠寶公司生產的首飾腕錶

With the aim of stimulating the design of contemporary diamond jewellery for everyday wear for today's modern women, De Beers Diamond Information Centre held a jewellery design contest in 1994. The price of the articles designed was to be within the range of US$500/1,500 each. The result was highly successful with the participation of more than 500 contestants. A number of creative designs were submitted and received Certificates of Merit. Five winners were awarded a trophy each from De Beers.

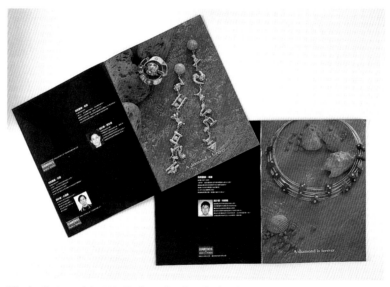

Winning Designs of the 1994 De Beers Jewellery Design Contest
1994年鑽飾設計比賽的優勝作品

為了推動今日現代女性日常配帶鑽石首飾，戴比爾斯鑽石諮詢中心在1994年舉辦了一個首飾設計比賽，每件參賽作品的價格必須在500至1,500美元之間。這項比賽吸引了超過500名參賽者，成績令人相當滿意，不少參賽作品的設計極具創意，獲大會頒發獎狀。五名優勝者分別獲戴比爾斯頒發獎座。

In view of the success, it was decided to hold the 1995 Diamond for Modern Women Design Competition (D F M W D C) jointly with the Diamond Importers Association (DIA) who have for the last 21 years supported and sponsored their own jewellery design competition. The contest was also expanded to include all the East Asian markets. A total of 643 entries from 12 countries were received. The final judging will be held in late 1995 in Hong Kong. Competition of this nature has provided vast support to enhance the design of jewellery articles produced in Hong Kong.

The Prize Presentation of the 1994 DFMWDC
1994年鑽飾設計比賽頒獎禮

鑑於該項比賽成績美滿,大會決定聯同鑽石入口商會合辦1995年新女性鑽飾設計比賽。在過去21年,鑽石入口商會均自行舉辦首飾設計比賽。這項比賽亦擴大參賽範圍至所有東亞國家,共有來自12個國家的643名參賽者報名參加,最後評選定於1995年底在香港舉行。這類比賽為香港的首飾產品提供大量設計靈感及推動力。

The Manufacturing Plant of Myer Jewelry Mfr. Limited
萬雅珠寶公司的生產廠房

The Assembling Plant of Myer Jewelry Mfr. Limited
萬雅珠寶公司的鑲配廠房

Most of the jewellery manufacturers in Hong Kong are small to medium in size, employing 10 to 100 workers. However, some of the manufacturers also engage in the refining, retailing and export business and their operations are much larger in scale. Chow Sang Sang Holdings International Limited (CSSH), for example, is a publicly listed company and the CSSH group operates a jewellery manufacturing plant, an electrolytic gold refinery and a gold assay laboratory (under the Hong Kong Laboratory Accreditation Scheme). Additionally, the group owns 25 retail shops and has established a few subsidiary companies to undertake business transactions in the field of bullion, securities and futures dealing. Currently, more than 1,100 people are employed by the CSSH group.

The other jewellery companies which are listed in the Hong Kong Stock Exchange include Continental, King Fook, Fu Hui, Rhine and Tse Sui Luen. The number of establishments

香港大部分首飾製造商均屬中小型規模，僱用10至100名工人。然而，若干製造商亦參與冶煉、零售及出口業務，而經營規模亦較大。例如周生生集團國際有限公司（一間上市公司）便經營首飾鑲作工場、電解煉金廠及黃金鑑定實驗所（按香港實驗所認可計劃設立）。此外，該集團亦擁有25間零售店舖及成立數間附屬公司參與黃金、證券及期貨買賣。現時，周生生集團僱用1,100多名員工。

在香港聯交所上市的其他珠寶首飾公司有恒和、景福、福輝、萊利及謝瑞麟。全港有接近1,100間珠寶首飾公司，整個行業的就業人數（包括熟練與非熟練勞工）為12,000人左

A Chuk Kam Mahjong set produced by Chow Sang Sang Jewellery Co., Limited
周生生珠寶金行生產的足金麻雀

of the industry is close to 1,100 with a total workforce, comprising skilled and unskilled labour, of nearly 12,000. The majority of the manufacturing plants are operated by local Chinese people in Hong Kong. About 15 of the establishments are owned by overseas investors, mainly from Japan and USA.

The high quality of traditional Chinese craftsmanship is well accepted in the world. In the early stage of development of the jewellery industry in Hong Kong, handcraft was the main manufacturing process. However, the technique continues to improve with the support of rapid infrastructure development in Hong Kong.

Since the mid 1970's, the technology has greatly advanced through joint-venture projects with foreign institutions specializing in the field of jewellery manufacture. Most of the jewellers in Hong Kong now apply various techniques of die-casting and stamping for mass production. Vacuum

右。大部分製造商為香港的本地華人，由海外投資者經營的首飾廠約15間，主要來自日本及美國。

中國精湛的傳統手工藝，早已得到世界各地讚賞。香港的金飾業在發展初期，生產主要是靠手工製造。隨着香港金飾市場的迅速發展，生產技術已不斷提升。

自七零年代中開始，港商與專門製造首飾的外國機構合作經營，使製造技術大幅提升。香港很多首飾製造商現已應用壓鑄、冲壓等技術作大量生產，此外亦採用真空鑄造及電鑄方法生產精巧的空心金飾及配飾，藉以減低飾物的重量。

Chuk Kam Statues of 18 "Monks" produced by King Fook Gold & Jewellery Co., Limited
景福珠寶鐘錶公司生產的足金十八羅漢像

Chuk Kam Figurines representing Prosperity, Happiness and Longevity produced by Chow Tai Fook Jewellery Co., Limited　周大福珠寶金行生產的足金福祿壽像

93

casting and electroforming are employed to produce precise hollow gold jewellery and adornments in order to reduce the weight of the article.

The Hong Kong Productivity Council has recently developed a process for electroforming pure gold for the production of chuk kam articles in one piece without any soldering. This process is best applicable to making traditional Chinese statues. Chuk kam figurines representing prosperity, happiness and longevity, for example, can be produced more efficiently by an electroforming process.

The combination of traditional Chinese craftsmanship and modern technology has greatly improved the quality of jewellery production in Hong Kong. This is one of the key factors contributing to the success of the industry.

In order to exercise more stringent quality control, the Trade Descriptions Ordinance was enacted by the Government in 1981. The Ordinance makes special reference to goldware with the following key clause:

香港生產力促進局最近發展出一個電鑄純金的工序，可以原件生產無焊口的足金飾物，這工序最適宜用作鑄造各種中國傳統足金擺件，例如利用電鑄工序便可更具效率地生產「福、祿、壽」足金像。

中國傳統手工藝與現代科技的結合，大大地提高了香港製造珠寶首飾的質量，也是該行業成功的一個重要因素。

為了更嚴格控制金飾的品質，政府於1981年制訂的《商品說明條例》中，特別對金飾作出以下規定：

Chuk Kam Jewellery produced by Just Gold Co., Limited
鎮金店生產的足金首飾

"A trade description which indicates any articles (other than an article of pure gold) is of gold shall be a false trade description unless the article consists solely of gold alloy and (i) contains not less than 8 carats of gold; or (ii) bears a mark clearly indicating in carats by number or by number and the letters "k", "c", or "ct", the fineness of the gold content; or (iii) bears a mark clearly indicating in parts per thousand the fineness of the gold content."

A schedule to the Ordinance defines the fineness of gold equivalent to each number of carats. Steps were taken in the mid 1990s to review the feasibility of marking each individual piece of jewellery and to introduce a compulsory hallmarking system which will enhance Hong Kong's position as one of the leading jewellery manufacturing centres in the world.

「除非製品是完全由黃金合金製成，並符合下列規定的一項，否則任何表示該製品是由黃金製成（千足純金製成品除外）的商品說明均屬虛假商品說明：(i) 黃金含量不少於 8 克拉；或 (ii) 附有清晰地以數字或數字連同英文字母 "k"、"c" 或 "ct" 來表示其黃金成色標誌；或 (iii) 附有清晰地以黃金在一千份合金裏面所佔份數來表示其黃金成色的標誌。」

該條例的附表更訂明每克拉的黃金成色。政府在九零年代中更採取步驟，研究推行在首飾上加蓋黃金純度印記規定的可行性。有了這個制度，香港作為世界珠寶首飾製造中心的地位將會大大提高。

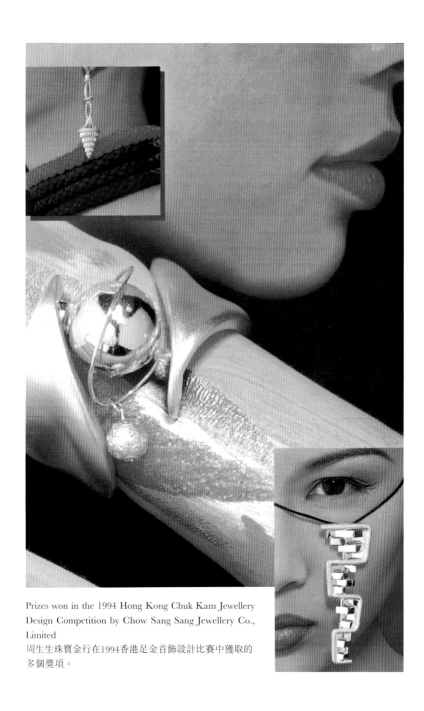

Prizes won in the 1994 Hong Kong Chuk Kam Jewellery
Design Competition by Chow Sang Sang Jewellery Co.,
Limited
周生生珠寶金行在1994香港足金首飾設計比賽中獲取的
多個獎項。

In the United Kingdom, for instance, it is required by law that gold wares must be made in one of the legal standards of fineness and must be hallmarked by the Assay Offices. The authorized standards are 22, 18, 14 and 9 carats of fine gold in every 24 parts. Given below are some of the British standard hallmarks.

22 carat gold 22克拉金   18 carat gold 18克拉金

14 carat gold 14克拉金   9 carat gold 9克拉金

London   Birmingham   Sheffield   Edinburgh
倫敦   伯明翰   夏菲爾德   愛丁堡

British Hallmarks on Gold Articles   英國鑑定黃金純度標記

Since the beginning of the current decade, manufacturing facilities have been established in China by jewellers in

以英國為例，法例規定金器必須遵守其中一項法定成色標準鑄造，並經成色鑑定機構檢定蓋印。法定標準為每24份含22、18、14及9份純金。以上是數款代表不同克拉黃金純度的標記。

自九零年代初，香港不少珠寶首飾製造商在中國大陸設廠，希望藉較低廉的勞工來增強出口競爭力。然而，在多項因素

Hong Kong in order to take advantage of the lower labour costs and to increase the competitiveness of the export trade. However, this establishment is limited to the production of jewellery articles in the lower price range due to a number of factors, particularly in the field of infrastructure development.

With the objective of improving manufacturing skills, the World Gold Council has been actively organizing seminars and training courses for jewellers in Greater China (China, Taiwan and Hong Kong). In 1994, the Council held separate seminars in these places to introduce the 1994-95 Asian Gold Trends. Specialists from Italy were invited to conduct these functions.

To further extend the programme, a design competition for chuk kam jewellery was held in Hong Kong, Taiwan and China individually. The winners of these contests were then invited to participate in the 1994 Asian Chuk Kam Jewellery Design Competition. The result was highly successful.

影響下,特別是各種基建設施的不足,這些工廠現時多數生產較低價的K金首飾。

為協助提高中國的金飾製造技術,世界黃金協會積極為中國、台灣及香港的珠寶首飾製造商籌辦研討會及培訓課程。1994年,該會在三地分別舉行講座,介紹1994-95年亞洲金飾趨勢。大會邀請了來自意大利的專家主持這些講座。

為進一步推廣這個計劃,該會分別在香港、台灣及中國舉辦了足金首飾設計比賽,優勝者獲邀請參加1994年度亞洲足金首飾設計比賽,成績非常美滿。

The export boom of gold jewellery made in Hong Kong has continued unabated since the early 1980s and jewellery manufacture has become the sixth largest industry in the territory. Details covering the domestic exports of jewellery articles from Hong Kong to various countries in the world in 1993 and 1994 are contained in the table appended below.

HK$'000（千港元計）

Country 國家	1993	1994
USA 美國	2,572,000	2,506,000
Japan 日本	1,225,000	1,375,000
Switzerland 瑞士	320,000	490,000
Germany Fed Rep 德國	407,000	350,000
France 法國	223,000	230,000
Singapore 新加坡	176,000	205,000
Taiwan 台灣	90,000	157,000
United Kingdom 英國	96,000	103,000
Australia 澳洲	55,000	91,000
China 中國	96,000	48,000
Others 其他	566,000	603,000
Total 總值	5,826,000	6,158,000

Source : Census and Statistics Department, Hong Kong Government
資料來源： 香港政府統計處

自八零年代初起，香港的金飾出口業一直保持蓬勃，首飾製造業躍升為第六大出口工業。上表為1993及1994年香港輸往世界各國金飾統計數字。

In respect of the local consumer market in Hong Kong, the infrastructure for marketing and distributing different categories of products has been well developed. Hundreds of retailing shops are established in the island of Hong Kong, Kowloon and the New Territories. Chow Sang Sang, Chow Tai Fook, Debera Jewellery, Henry Jewellery, Just Gold, King Fook, Lane Crawford, Larry Jewellery and Tse Sui Luen are currently the most active suppliers.

Most of the shops are open until 9.00 p.m. daily and provide excellent service to customers. Through the extensive sales network, jewellery products are sold to local residents in Hong Kong and visiting tourists from different parts of the world. According to the Hong Kong Tourist Association (HKTA), jewellery is the second most popular consumer item bought by tourists visiting Hong Kong. In 1993 sales amounted to HK$5,710 million which occupied 9.8% of total spending by visitors. The value continued to increase in 1994 and totalled HK$6,900 million.

在香港本地零售市場方面，各類金飾製品的宣傳推廣及分銷網絡已極為發達，在港島、九龍及新界各區的金飾店數以百計，而目前以周生生、周大福、戴寶樂、鎮科、鎮金店、景福、連卡佛、俊文及謝瑞麟為市場上最活躍的供應商。

大部分金飾店每天均營業至晚上九時，為顧客提供優良服務。透過廣闊的銷售網絡，首飾製品的銷售對象除香港本地居民外，還有來自世界各地的遊客。根據香港旅遊協會（「旅協」）的資料，珠寶首飾是訪港旅客的第二大消費項目，1993年的銷售額便達57.1億港元，佔旅客總消費額的9.8%，這數字在1994年持續上升，總值達69億港元。

Despite accelerating inflation, Hong Kong remains a competitive place for tourists. In 1994, 9.3 million visitors came to Hong Kong and spent a total of HK$62,500 million, an increase of 7.1 per cent over the record in 1993. Spending by tourists from China increased substantially in the year and amounted to HK$10,600 million. Taiwan remained on the top of the list with a total spending of HK$13,800 million. Breakdown details of spending by visitors from different parts of the world are given in the following table:

儘管通脹不斷上升，外國遊客仍視香港為旅遊勝地。1994年，訪港旅客達930萬人次，總消費額625億港元，較1993年消費上升7.1%。年內中國旅客的消費顯著上升，達106億港元。台灣旅客的消費最高，達138億港元。世界各地旅客訪港的消費分析列表如下：

HK$ Million（百萬港元計）

Country 國家	1993		1994	
	Amount 消費額	%	Amount 消費額	%
Taiwan 台灣	13,900	23.9	13,800	22.1
Japan 日本	10,100	17.3	12,200	19.5
China 中國	8,000	13.7	10,600	17.0
Southeast Asia 東南亞	8,400	14.4	8,000	12.7
West Europe 西歐	5,900	10.1	6,200	9.9
USA/Canada 美國/加拿大	6,200	10.6	5,600	9.0
Australia/NZ 澳洲/紐西蘭	1,900	3.3	1,900	3.0
Others 其他	3,900	6.8	4,200	6.7
Total 總額	58,300	100.0	62,500	100.0

Source : Hong Kong Tourist Association
資料來源： 香港旅遊協會

One of the retailing shops of Larry Jewellery Co., Limited
俊文寶石店門市部之一

One of the retailing shops of Chow Tai Fook Jewellery Co., Limited
周大福珠寶金行門市部之一

Statistics released by HKTA also revealed that money spent on shopping by tourists accounted for more than 50% of the total spending. In 1994, the per capita spending by Japanese, Taiwanese and Mainland Chinese visitors continued to increase and amounted to HK$8,444, HK$8,311 and HK$5,469 respectively. The trend indicated that the consumption of gold jewellery by tourists from the above countries, particularly China, stepped up considerably in 1994.

In order to increase the confidence of the consumers, members of HKTA (members only) are entitled to display the logo (below) of the association in their shops. The logo signifies members' commitment to provident good service and value and upholding certain ethical standards.

旅協公布的統計數字亦顯示遊客在購物方面佔總消費的50%以上。在1994年，日本、台灣及中國大陸遊客的人均消費持續上升，分別達8,444港元、8,311港元及5,469港元，這趨勢顯示1994年以上國家（特別是中國）的遊客在香港購買金飾的消費額顯著上升。

為增強消費者的信心，只有旅協會員才可以在店內張貼這個會徽（上圖），表示該商店符合商業操守，以合理價格為顧客提供優良服務。

The higher spending of Asian tourists visiting Hong Kong has boosted the offtake of chuk kam jewellery and adornments. These products are sold at the fine gold prices fixed every morning by the Hong Kong Jewellers' and Goldsmiths' Association plus manufacturing charges which are relatively low, averaged at about 8% over the intrinsic value of gold. Over the last few years, chuk kam jewellery articles made with more innovative designs and better finish have been gaining popularity, particularly among the younger population in Hong Kong. Despite the considerably higher mark-up, ranging from 20% to 30% above the gold price, overall sales of these products have been increasing steadily.

The official domestic exports and local sales of jewellery products manufactured in Hong Kong amounted to HK$12,400 million in 1994, making useful contribution to the Gross Domestic Product of Hong Kong. It is beyond doubt that the existing establishment of the industry will foster further growth in the years ahead.

亞洲區遊客在香港的較高消費力,促使香港足金首飾及配飾銷路日益蓬勃,這些足金首飾均以香港珠石玉器金銀首飾業商會每天早上所報兩金價,加頗為相宜的鑲工(平均約8%左右)買賣。在過去數年,時款及手工精美的足金首飾漸趨流行,特別受年青一代的消費者歡迎。雖然產品賣價一般高出兩金價20%至30%,但銷量仍穩步增長。

1994年香港製造的首飾製品本地出口及零售總值達124億港元,對香港的生產總值有重大貢獻,而現時香港金飾業發展的規模,對未來增長奠下鞏固的根基。

FUTURE PROSPECTS 展望

Hong Kong has achieved its status as a leading regional gold centre on the strength of a long history and solid background in the field of trading and manufacturing. Economic growth in China will, on the other hand, provide further support to the future development of the gold market in Hong Kong.

At this stage, the gold market in China remains highly restricted. Pricing, fabrication, imports and exports of gold and gold-related products, and the supply of gold to local manufacturing industries are under strict government control. Foreign participation in the Chinese gold trade is forbidden and only a limited number of foreign corporations have entered into joint ventures with Chinese enterprises in the field of manufacturing and mining.

The galloping economic growth in the last decade greatly boosted per capita income in China, particularly for those

香港在黃金貿易及製造金飾有悠久的歷史及穩固的基礎，因而成為亞太區的黃金中心。另一方面，中國的經濟增長，將繼續推動香港黃金市場的發展。

現時中國的黃金市場仍然受到很大限制。無論是黃金及有關產品在定價、加工、進出口，或在國內金飾製造業的黃金供應方面，均受政府嚴格控制。當局禁止外資參與中國的黃金業，只有少數外資公司與中國企業在國內組成合營公司，從事金飾製造及開採金礦業務。

過去十年來，中國急劇的經濟增長大大提高了人均收入，尤其是私營企業經營者的收入增長更大。在改革開放初期，人民多將增加了的收入購置基本家庭用品。但在滿足了這方面

running the privately-owned enterprises. During the first phase of the evolution, the increased earnings were spent in the accumulation of basic household goods but consumer preference has switched to more luxurious items including fashion wear, watches, cigarette lighters and gold jewellery. So far as gold jewellery is concerned, the initial demand was relatively small focusing on chuk kam adornments with simple designs. However, since the beginning of the current decade, consumption has greatly increased as wealth is building up among a wider cross-section of the population.

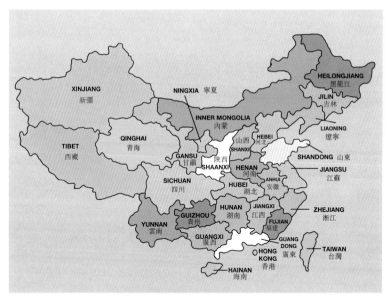

The Map of Greater China（China, Taiwan, Hong Kong）
大中華（中國、台灣、香港）地理圖

的需要後，消費者便會購買更多時裝、手錶、打火機及金飾等奢侈品。初時，金飾的需求並不大，主要是設計簡單的小巧足金首飾。但踏入九十年代後，隨着更多人民累積較多財富，金飾的購買量便急速增長。

The population distribution in China is uneven and the per capita GDP differs vastly from one province to another. There are 31 provinces, municipalities and autonomous regions in China. This disparate economic growth greatly influences consumer preference and determines affordability of gold products in different provinces. China is not a homogeneous market as far as gold jewellery articles are concerned. While consumers in the Special Economic Zones along the south-eastern coast of the Mainland are more fashion minded and sophisticated, the demand in the less prosperous provinces focuses more on basic chuk kam ornaments and small bars.

Consumption of gold and gold jewellery in the Mainland reached an unexpected high level of 420 tonnes in 1992 although the quantity declined following the launch of the austerity measures in 1993. Current offtake is in the region of 230 tonnes.

中國的人口分布並不平均，省與省之間的人均國民生產值差別極大。全中國有31個省、市及自治區。不同省份經濟增長的高低，對人民的消費能力及消費者的愛好都有差距。就金飾而言，中國並非一個均一的市場，東南沿海一帶經濟特區的消費者比較喜愛時尚潮流的金飾，而在發展較慢的內陸地區，則以傳統款式的足金首飾及小型金條較受歡迎。

1992年，中國的黃金及金飾購買量高達420公噸，雖然購買量在1993年已隨着緊縮政策的實施而回落，但現時仍然維持在每年230公噸的水平。

The economic and social reforms in China will continue and development and growth will gain momentum after a period of adjustment and consolidation. It is evident that the majority of the 1.2 billion people in China are prepared to strive for a better life. The continuation of the opening up of the country and the move towards market socialism will provide these people with ample opportunities.

While looking at current developments in China, it should be remembered that Hong Kong was just a rocky island in 1841 when Great Britain took over the administration of the Colony. With practically no natural resources, it is remarkable that Hong Kong has now been established as one of the world's most successful city states. The "laissez – faire" policy which the government employs, coupled with the flexibility, adaptability and hard-working nature of the Chinese people in Hong Kong, have contributed vastly to the success.

中國的經濟及社會改革將會持續,而經過一段調整及鞏固期後,發展和增長步伐將會更快。中國的十二億人口中,大部分都希望爭取更佳的生活水平。隨着中國繼續開放,步向社會主義市場經濟,人民將獲得大量改善生活的機會。

中國現今的發展,使我們想起在1841年由英國接手管治時,香港只是一個荒蕪的小島,雖然缺乏天然資源,香港現已發展成為世界最繁榮的城市之一。政府採取的「不干預」政策,連同居港華人的靈活性、適應力強及勤奮特質,對香港取得今天的地位貢獻良多。

The sovereignty of Hong Kong will be returned to China in 1997 when the legal status of Hong Kong will be changed to a Special Administration Region (SAR) of China. The governor of the future SAR government will be appointed by China but Hong Kong will operate with its own laws and with its own legislative assembly. While there remain various issues to be addressed and resolved, the return of the sovereignty of Hong Kong to China will be in accordance with the Joint Declaration formalized by China and Great Britain in 1984.

During the interim period, local entrepreneurs in the business community in Hong Kong continue their undertaking in various fields with full confidence. Foreign investment is well maintained with Japan and the USA being the largest investors in the manufacturing industries in Hong Kong. Infrastructure projects are being developed in the territory by the government independently or jointly with the private sector in order to cope with the environments and growth beyond 1997.

香港的主權於1997年回歸中國後，香港在法律上便成為中國的特別行政區，未來特別行政區政府的首長將由中國委任，但香港仍保留本身的法律制度，設有立法會組織。雖然中英雙方尚有不少問題需要商議解決，香港的主權將按1984年的中英聯合聲明移交中國。

在過渡期間，香港工商界人士仍信心十足地繼續他們不同行業的投資及運作。外商繼續在香港投資，而日本及美國是現時香港製造業的最大投資者。政府現正積極獨資或與私營機構合作發展基建工程，以應付現時及1997年以後發展的需要。

The Airport Core Programme (ACP), for instance, is the largest project which will cost a total of HK\$158 billion to complete. The programme consists of 10 inter-linked projects which are focused on the construction of a new airport at Chek Lap Kok to replace Hong Kong's existing airport, along with 34 kilometers of new highways, a railway, more than 350 hectares of land reclamation and a new town.

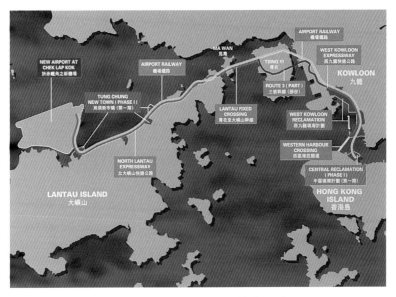

Airport Core Programme Projects, Hong Kong　香港機場核心工程

例如，機場核心工程是現時香港最大型的基建工程，總投資額高達1,580億港元，包括10個相連的工程項目，主要工程是在赤鱲角興建一個新機場以取代香港現有的機場，連同34公里長的新幹線、一條鐵路、超過350公頃的填海土地及一個新市鎮。

With regard to the bullion industry, the market in the territory will be further extended when Hong Kong becomes part of China in 1997. Chinese people have great affinity for gold. However, the existing per capita ownership remains exceedingly low at an estimated 1.5 grams. The acquisition of ornamental and investment gold jewellery by the people in the Mainland will accelerate on the strength of higher

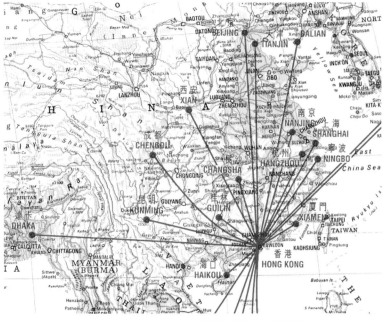

Route Map of Dragon Airlines, Hong Kong　香港港龍航空公司航線圖

1997年香港回歸中國後，香港的黃金市場將會進一步擴展。中國人熱愛黃金，但現時中國十二億人民的人均黃金擁有量仍遠遠偏低，估計約為1.5克左右。相信隨着國內生產總值的增長，中國人民購買金飾作裝飾及保值用途的趨勢將會不

GDP growth. This development will increase the level of activities in the gold market in China and will provide further support to Hong Kong in enhancing its role as an international gold centre. Aside from the free enterprise environment and the infrastructure already developed as one of the major financial centres in the world, Hong Kong is at the geographical centre of Asia and is poised to become the gateway to China.

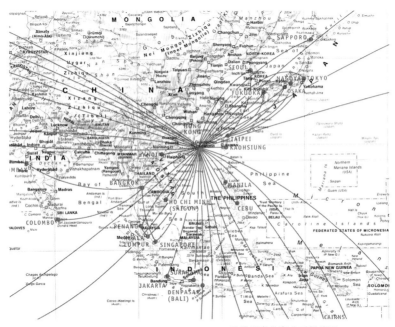

Route Map of Cathay Pacific Airways, Hong Kong　　香港國泰航空公司航線圖

斷增加，這種發展將會令國內黃金市場更趨蓬勃，有助加強香港在未來數年的國際黃金中心地位。香港擁有自由貿易制度及完善基建設施，因而成為世界主要金融中心之一，除此之外，香港位於亞洲區心臟地帶，將會成為通往中國的貿易門戶。

APPENDICES 附錄

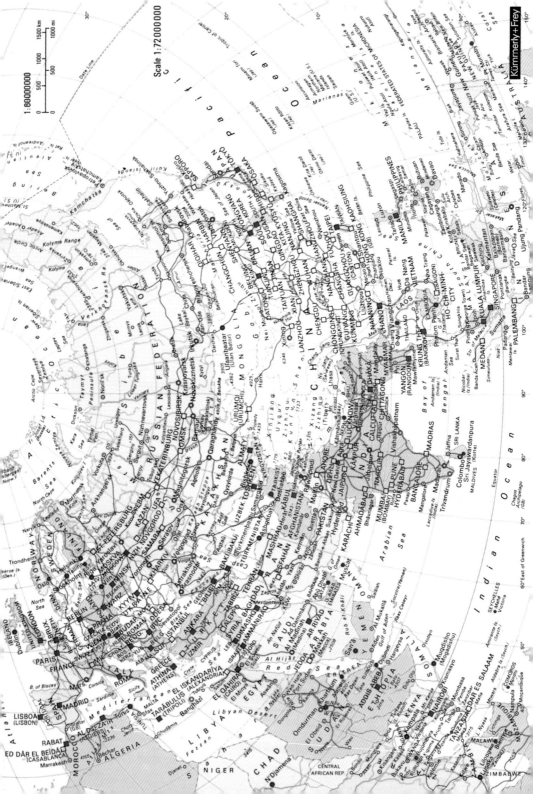

MAIN FEATURES OF KEY ASIAN GOLD MARKETS 亞洲主要黃金市場特點

Country 國家	Market Status 市場情況		1994 Offtake 1994年購買量	1994 Imports 1994年進口量	Acceptable Melters & Assayers 國際認許的熔鑄及鑑定機構 (Good Delivery Bars) 國際認許金條
	Loco London Gold Trading 本地倫敦金買賣	Import of Gold Bars 金條進口	Kilos 公斤	Kilos 公斤	
China 中國	Restricted 限制	Restricted 限制	224,000	–	Refinery of China
Hong Kong 香港	Free 自由	Free 自由	47,500	326,100	Nil 無
India 印度	Restricted 限制	Restricted 限制	415,000	250,000	Nil 無
Indonesia 印尼	Free 自由	Free 自由	97,000	80,000	Nil 無
Japan 日本	Free 自由	Free 自由	229,000	197,300	Ishifuku Metal Industry Co Ltd. / Mitsubishi Materials Corporation / Mitsui Mining & Smelting Co Ltd / Nippon Mining Co Ltd / Sumitomo Metal Mining Co Ltd / Tanaka Kikinzoku Kogyo K.K. / Tokuriki Honten & Co Ltd
Korea, North 北韓	Restricted 限制	Restricted 限制	–	–	Central Bank, Democratic People's Republic of Korea
Korea, South 南韓	Restricted 限制	Free 自由	106,000	50,000	Nil 無
Malaysia 馬來西亞	Free 自由	Free 自由	25,000	40,000	Nil 無
Myanmar 緬甸	Restricted 限制	Restricted 限制	17,000	17,000	Nil 無
Philippines 菲律賓	Restricted 限制	Restricted 限制	2,800	–	Central Bank of the Philippines
Singapore 新加坡	Free 自由	Free 自由	24,000	281,000	Degussa (Private) Limited
Taiwan 台灣	Restricted 限制	Free 自由	162,000	116,000	Nil 無
Thailand 泰國	Restricted 限制	Free 自由	124,000	25,000	Nil 無
Vietnam 越南	Restricted 限制	Free 自由	28,000	28,000	Nil 無

Sources : World Gold Council; Standard London (Asia) Limited, Hong Kong
資料來源 : 世界黃金協會；英國標旗（亞洲）有限公司，香港

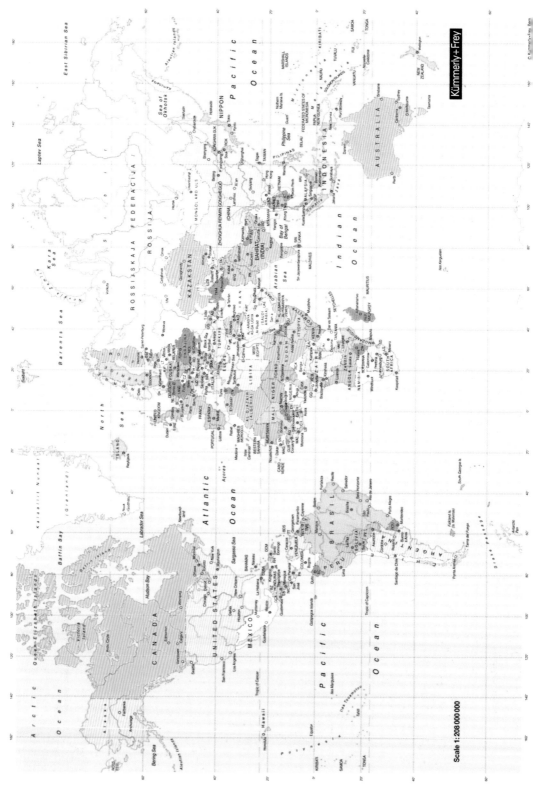

LONDON GOLD & SILVER PRICE 倫敦金銀價

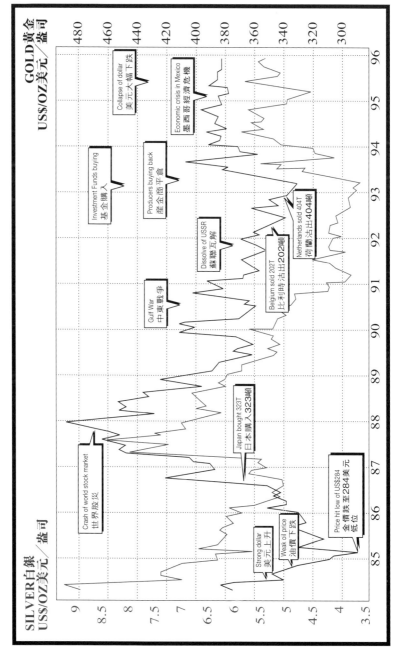

Sources : Reuters, Hong Kong; Standard London (Asia) Limited, Hong Kong
資料來源 : 路透社，香港；英國標旗（亞洲）有限公司，香港

International Monetary
Fund (IMF) Headquarters,
Washington, D. C., U.S.A.
國際貨幣基金會總部，美
國華盛頓

WORLD CENTRAL BANK GOLD RESERVES 世界中央銀行黃金儲備

Country 國家	1970 Quantity Tonnes 數量 公噸	1970 As % of Total Reserve 佔總儲備 %	1980 Quantity Tonnes 數量 公噸	1980 As % of Total Reserve 佔總儲備 %	1990 Quantity Tonnes 數量 公噸	1990 As % of Total Reserve 佔總儲備 %	1994 Quantity Tonnes 數量 公噸	1994 As % of Total Reserve 佔總儲備 %
Industrial IMF Countries 國際貨幣基金會工業國								
United States 美國	9,838	77.6	8,221	90.9	8,146	58.3	8,149	61.3
Germany 德國	3,537	30.6	2,961	53.6	2,961	35.1	2,960	32.0
Switzerland 瑞士	2,426	54.8	2,591	75.8	2,591	52.3	2,591	47.9
France 法國	3,138	72.5	2,547	63.8	2,547	46.1	2,550	54.4
Italy 意大利	2,566	55.6	2,075	63.6	2,075	29.0	2,075	44.2
Netherlands 荷蘭	1,589	56.8	1,366	69.0	1,366	49.2	1,082	27.8
Belgium 比利時	1,306	53.3	1,064	72.0	939	48.9	779	40.9
Japan 日本	473	11.7	753	36.7	753	10.6	753	6.9
Austria 奧地利	635	42.2	656	70.2	635	45.6	580	29.4
United Kingdom 英國	1,198	49.3	585	35.0	588	16.9	574	14.7
Canada 加拿大	703	17.8	653	80.3	460	24.2	166	10.8
Australia 澳洲	212	14.9	246	73.4	246	15.8	246	21.1
Developing IMF Countries 國際貨幣基金會發展中國家								
Africa 非洲	896	29.6	656	39.5	376	22.1	395	20.0
Middle East 中東	936	24.1	1,101	22.8	1,154	21.5	1,077	19.5
Other Western 其他西方國家	1,166	21.6	1,409	37.1	1,344	20.1	1,266	11.2
Asia 亞洲	622	12.4	1,160	36.7	1,627	10.0	1,699	6.2
TOTAL 合計	**31,241**	**41.3**	**28,044**	**57.8**	**27,808**	**28.6**	**26,942**	**23.8**

Source （資料來源）：International Monetary Fund, Washington, D. C. 國際貨幣基金會，華盛頓

Gold Mining
金礦開採

WORLD GOLD MINE PRODUCTION 世界金礦年產量

Tonnes 公噸

Region/Country 地區／國家	1981	1991	1992	1993	1994
Africa 非洲	697.40	689.80	714.20	729.80	698.80
North America 北美洲	97.00	471.70	490.50	485.40	477.10
Asia 亞洲	90.90	265.30	308.10	317.30	323.30
Oceania & Australasia 大洋洲及澳大利西亞	36.80	246.50	257.80	262.20	270.30
Latin America 拉丁美洲	104.00	210.10	214.90	229.10	252.20
Soviet Union & Other CIS 蘇聯及其他獨聯體國家	262.00	252.00	13.50	17.60	19.80
Russia 俄羅斯	0.00	0.00	162.10	175.50	164.70
Uzbekistan 烏茲別克	0.00	0.00	64.50	66.60	64.40
Europe 歐洲	14.90	32.20	25.30	25.60	25.50
Total 合計	1,303.00	2,167.60	2,250.90	2,309.10	2,296.10

Source（資料來源）：Gold Fields Mineral Services Limited, London　黃金礦業服務有限公司，倫敦

Chuk Kam Train Set produced by Chow Sang Sang
周生生製造的足金火車模形

WORLD GOLD SUPPLY AND DEMAND 世界黃金供求量

Tonnes 公噸

	1981	1991	1992	1993	1994
Supply 供應					
Mine production 金礦產量	1,268	2,168	2,251	2,309	2,296
Net official sales 官方淨銷量	(276)	118	604	488	86
Old gold scrap 舊金廢料	244	463	467	552	593
Forward sales 期貨銷售	–	96	164	214	122
Option hedging 期權對冲	–	14	103	–	23
Implied disinvestment 遞減投資量	275	261	–	–	199
Total Supply 總供應量	**1,511**	**3,120**	**3,589**	**3,563**	**3,319**
Demand 需求					
Jewellery manufacture 金飾製造	798	2,312	2,710	2,517	2,576
Electronics fabrication 電子產品加工	93	206	176	182	192
Other fabrication 其他加工	346	305	271	305	266
Bar hoarding 金條囤積	274	252	282	163	233
Gold loans 借金	–	45	85	65	52
Option hedging 期權對冲	–	–	–	31	–
Implied investment 投資量	–	–	65	300	–
Total Demand 總需求量	**1,511**	**3,120**	**3,589**	**3,563**	**3,319**

Source (資料來源)：Gold Fields Mineral Services Limited, London 黃金礦業服務有限公司，倫敦

Silverware
銀器

WORLD SILVER SUPPLY AND DEMAND 世界白銀供求量

Million Ounces 百萬盎司

	1990	1991	1992	1993	1994
Supply 供應					
Mine production 銀礦產量	514.2	504.6	499.4	468.4	444.2
Official sector sales 官方銷量	11.0	11.5	8.1	13.8	32.4
Old silver scrap 舊銀廢料	114.2	120.6	124.7	128.6	132.5
Hedging 對冲	15.2	22.9	—	23.6	—
Implied disinvestment 遞減投資量	28.8	21.7	82.0	126.7	150.2
Total Supply 總供應量	**683.4**	**681.2**	**714.2**	**761.1**	**759.3**
Demand 需求					
Industrial & decorative 工業及裝飾	263.5	270.8	268.8	263.7	279.4
Photography 攝影	219.2	213.7	212.6	212.9	219.3
Jewellery & silverware 首飾及銀器	168.1	168.5	197.8	244.7	208.3
Official coins 官方鑄幣	31.6	28.1	33.3	39.5	42.9
Other fabrication 其他加工	—	—	—	—	—
Hedging 對冲	—	—	1.7	—	9.9
Total Demand 總需求量	**683.4**	**681.2**	**714.2**	**761.1**	**759.3**

Source （資料來源）: The Silver Institute, Washington, D. C. 白銀協會，華盛頓

MAJOR HISTORICAL EVENTS RELATING TO THE MONETARY ROLE OF GOLD
歷史上黃金的貨幣角色

PRE NINETEEN SIXTIES 一九六零年代前

- Gold has been used as a means of exchange for over 3,000 years. In China it was first legalized as a medium of circulation in 1091 BC. In the West, the introduction of gold coins is generally credited to the Lydian king Croesus (561-546 BC). This evolved slowly into the Gold Standard, which became the basis of Britain's monetary system in 1717 and was more widely adopted in Europe in the last years of the 19th century. The United States went onto the Gold Standard in 1900. Under the Gold Standard the price of gold was fixed, and gold coins either formed the whole circulation of currency within a country or combined with notes which were redeemable in gold. Internationally, free import and export of gold meant that balance of payments deficits were settled in the metal; gold flowed out of a country in deficit, into a country in surplus.

黃金作為交易的媒介已有三千多年歷史。遠在公元前1091年，黃金在中國率先成為合法流通貨幣；而在西方國家，一般認為是利地亞末代國王克羅伊斯（公元前561-546年）首先鑄造金幣作為貨幣。經過一段漫長時期，金本位制度逐漸確立，在1717年成為英國貨幣制度的基礎，至十九世紀末期，歐洲國家已廣泛實行金本位制度。美國於1900年實行金本位制度。在這個制度下，黃金價格是固定的，而只有金幣或連同可兌換黃金的紙幣成為國家唯一的流通貨幣。在國際方面，黃金自由進出口，用以結算國際收支差額；黃金由收支出現逆差的國家流入收支出現順差的國家。

- On the outbreak of World War I, the Gold Standard was largely suspended because countries at war could not accept its disciplines and kept gold for vital war needs. Britain itself officially suspended the Gold Standard in 1919, but returned to a Gold Bullion Standard in 1926 under which notes could only be exchanged for 400 ounce good delivery bars. However, the economic turmoil of the early 1930s forced most nations off gold (Britain in 1931, the United States in 1933). Only movement of gold between central banks and governments was permitted. This created the Dollar Exchange Standard under which dollars could be traded for gold at the Federal Reserve. This system was confirmed by the Bretton Woods Agreement in 1944 and lasted until 1971.

第一次世界大戰爆發後，由於交戰各國不再遵守金本位制度的規範，將黃金保留作軍事用途，令該制度名存實亡。1919年，英國正式停止採用金本位制度，但於1926年恢復使用金磚本位制度；在這個制度下，紙幣只能兌換400盎司國際認許金條。然而，踏入1930年代初，世界經濟處於動盪時期，迫使大部分國家放棄以黃金兌換貨幣的制度（英國在1931年、美國在1933年），只容許中央銀行及各政府之間進行黃金交易活動。在這情況下，便形成了美元兌換制度，使美元可以在聯邦儲備局兌換黃金。國際間在1944年簽署了布雷頓森林協定，確認了這個制度，並一直實行至1971年。

- In 1934, President Roosevelt raised the official price at which the Federal Reserve would buy and sell gold to $35.00 an ounce, a level which the United States and European Central Banks struggled to maintain until 1968.

  1934年，美國總統羅斯福將聯邦儲備局買賣黃金的官價升至每盎司35美元，聯邦儲備局與歐洲的中央銀行一直致力維持這個兌換價，直至1968年。

IN NINETEEN SIXTY　一九六零年期間

- Due to growing demand in the free market for gold for jewellery and investment, the Gold Pool was formed by the USA together with Britain, Belgium, France, Italy, Netherlands, West Germany and Switzerland, with the intention of keeping the free market price close to the official parity of US$35.00 an ounce. This new set up was effectively an extension of the Exchange Stabilization Fund giving the Treasury the authority to increase the supply of gold in order to depress the free market price if necessary.

  由於自由市場對黃金作為製造首飾及投資用途的需求日增，美國聯同英國、比利時、法國、意大利、荷蘭、西德及瑞士成立黃金總庫，希望把黃金市價保持在接近官價每盎司35美元的水平。這個新機構實際上是外滙穩定基金的擴展，使財政部在必要時可增加黃金的供應量來壓抑自由市場的金價。

IN NINETEEN SIXTY EIGHT　一九六八年期間

- Central Banks suspended operations of the Gold Pool and the London Gold Market was closed for two weeks. This was a direct result of increasing worldwide speculation in gold due to an uncertain international monetary market and pressure on the US dollar after the TET Offensive in Vietnam.

由於國際貨幣市場呈現不穩及美元因美國陷入越戰而備受壓力，帶動全球黃金投機活動不斷增加。在此情況下，各國的中央銀行暫停黃金總庫的運作，而倫敦金市亦停市兩星期。

- During the closure of the London Gold Market, Credit Suisse, Swiss Bank Corporation and Union Bank of Switzerland formed the Pool in Zurich to undertake gold transactions. South Africa started regular gold sales through the Zurich Pool .

倫敦金市停業期間，瑞士信貸銀行、瑞士銀行及瑞士聯合銀行在蘇黎世成立金庫，進行黃金買賣。南非開始透過蘇黎世金庫定期沽售黃金。

- The Two-tier System was launched under which gold transacted in the private and official monetary sectors was handled separately.

黃金雙價制開始推行，將私人及官方黃金買賣分在兩個不同的市場進行。

IN NINETEEN SIXTY NINE　一九六九年期間

- Singapore liberalized the gold market for non-residents.

新加坡開放黃金市場予非當地居民。

- Restrictions covering imports of gold coins minted before 1934 were lifted in the USA.

美國解除對輸入1934年前鑄造的金幣的限制。

IN NINETEEN SEVENTY ONE　一九七一年期間

- Russia resumed selling gold to London, the first time since 1966.

  蘇聯自1966年停止出售黃金予倫敦以來，首次恢復向倫敦售金。

- The USA suspended gold convertibility of US dollar.

  美國宣布暫停以美元兌換黃金。

- President Nixon agreed at the Acoren Meeting to devalue US dollar. The Group of Ten agreed on the re-alignment of the parities with a devaluation of 7.89% for US dollar which turned the new official gold price to US$38.00 an ounce with variations of 2.25% each side.

  美國總統尼克遜在艾高連會議上，同意把美元貶值。十大工業國組織同意美元貶值7.89%，把黃金的新官價定為每盎司38美元，上下限波幅不超過2.25%。

IN NINETEEN SEVENTY THREE　一九七三年期間

- Japan liberalized gold imports.

  日本開放黃金進口。

- The US dollar was devalued for the second time and the official gold price was set at US$42.2222 an ounce.

  美元第二次貶值，黃金的官價定為每盎司42.2222美元。

- The official Two-tier System was discontinued.

  黃金雙價制終止。

- Singapore liberalized the gold market for residents.

  新加坡開放黃金市場予當地居民。

IN NINETEEN SEVENTY FOUR 一九七四年期間

- Hong Kong liberalized the gold market following the dissolution of the Sterling Area in 1972.

  繼1972年英鎊區解體後，香港開放黃金市場。

- EEC Finance Ministers reached the Zeist Accord under which Central Banks may trade gold between themselves at market related prices. If Central Banks buy gold from the free market, the effect of these operations should not be to increase their net gold holdings.

  歐洲共市財長達成宰斯特協議，各國中央銀行可按市價互相買賣黃金。如中央銀行從自由市場購入黃金，其數量不得用作增加中央銀行的淨持金量。

- Finance Ministers of the Group of Ten agreed that Central Banks may use their gold reserves as collateral at market related prices for foreign loans.

  十國財長同意中央銀行可用其黃金儲備，按市價計算作為外債的擔保。

- President Ford of the USA and President Giscard d'Estaing of France agreed that Central Banks may revalue their gold reserves at market related prices.

  美國總統福特及法國總統狄斯唐同意中央銀行可按市價重估其黃金儲備。

- The USA liberalized the gold market.

  美國開放黃金市場。

- US Treasury auctioned and sold 2.5 million ounces of gold.

  美國財政部拍賣250萬盎司黃金。

- UK suspended imports of gold coins issued after 1837 including Krugerrands.

  英國暫停輸入於1837年後發行的金幣，包括富格林金幣。

- The Group of Ten agreed that the Bank for International Settlements (BIS) can participate in the IMF auctions.

  十國組織同意國際結算銀行可參與國際貨幣基金會的拍賣。

- Members of IMF reached agreement to abandon the official gold price and to restitute 50% of gold to members at US$42.2222 an ounce. It was further agreed that Central Banks can buy and sell gold in the free market and that 1/6 of the IMF gold reserve was to be auctioned with the proceeds received used for helping under-developed countries.

  國際貨幣基金會成員達成協議，取消黃金官價制度，並以每盎司42.2222美元的價格，將一半黃金歸還各成員，同時協議中央銀行可在自由市場買賣黃金，而國際貨幣基金會將其六分一的黃金儲備拍賣，所得收入用來援助落後國家。

- The Group of Ten agreed not to buy gold in the free market before the revision of the IMF Articles of Association. However, they agreed that BIS can buy gold on their behalf.

  十國組織同意在國際貨幣基金會修訂組織章程前，不會在自由市場購入黃金，但卻同意國際結算銀行可代其購入黃金。

- Germany and Switzerland granted credit of US$250 million to Italy against collateral of gold. South Africa announced the overseas loan granted to them against collateral of 5 million ounces of gold.

  德國及瑞士批出2.50億美元的信貸予意大利，以黃金作抵押。南非宣布以500萬益司黃金作擔保，獲得外國貸款。

- The IMF commenced monthly auctions of gold which would continue for 4 years and 25 million ounces of gold would be offered for sale. They would also restitute a further 25 million ounces of gold to the member countries in the Fund.

  國際貨幣基金會開始每月拍賣黃金，為期四年，將共拍賣黃金2,500萬益司，另外又會把2,500萬益司的黃金歸還成員國。

NINETEEN EIGHTIES ONWARD　一九八零年代後

- The price reached the historical high of US$850 an ounce in 1980 but declined to the low of US$284 an ounce in 1985. The level of trading activities declined considerably in the decade but the physical offtake continued to accelerate, particularly in Asia. The status remains currently unchanged in major world gold markets.

1980年金價創歷史新高，升至每盎司850美元，到1985年則跌至每盎司284美元低位。八零年代黃金買賣活動大幅下降，但實金購買量持續增長，尤其以亞洲區為甚。這種市場狀況，目前在世界主要黃金市場繼續維持。

• Central Banks and central authorities were buyers and sellers of gold periodically in the 1980s and 1990s. The IMF "All Countries" gold holdings were 905.1 million ounces at end February 1995.

各國央行及政府當局在八零及九零年代均有購買或沽售黃金。國際貨幣基金會「全部成員國」黃金持有量於1995年2月底為9.051億盎司。

Standard London (Asia) Limited, Hong Kong
英國標旗（亞洲）有限公司，香港

TECHNICAL GUIDELINES
FOR ARBITRAGE DEALING
套戥交易技術指引

1. Should tael gold be long against loco London gold, US dollars are long. The corresponding amount of US dollars should be sold against HK dollars.

   如套戥倉是買入両金，沽出本地倫敦金，應將沽出本地倫敦金收取的美元沽出，兌換港元。

2. Should tael gold be short against loco London gold, US dollars are short. The corresponding amount of US dollars should be bought against HK dollars.

   如套戥倉是沽出両金，買入本地倫敦金，應以港元兌換買入本地倫敦金所需的美元。

3. Should the price go up against increasing open-interest, new buying is evident. The trend is bullish.

   如未平倉合約增加而價格向上走，市場走勢看好，有新買盤。

4. Should the price go down against increasing open-interest, new selling is evident. The trend is bearish.

   如未平倉合約增加而價格向下走，市場走勢看淡，有新沽盤。

5. Should the price go up against declining open-interest, shorts are off-setting. The situation is technically weak.

    如未平倉合約減少而價格向上走，顯示淡盤平倉，技術走勢示弱。

6. Should the price go down against declining open-interest, longs are squaring off. The situation is technically strong.

    如未平倉合約減少而價格向下走，顯示好盤平倉，技術走勢呈強。

7. Should the price go up against increasing volume, either shorts are squaring off or longs are buying. The trend is bullish.

    如交投量上升而價格向上走，可能是淡盤平倉或有新買盤，市場走勢看好。

8. Should the price go down against increasing volume, either longs are squaring off or shorts are selling. The trend is bearish.

    如交投量上升而價格向下走，可能是好盤平倉或有新沽盤，市場走勢看淡。

9. Should the price go up against declining volume, buying pressure is diminishing. A downside reaction is imminent.

    如交投量下降而價格向上走，顯示買盤逐漸減弱，跌勢可能出現。

10. Should the price go down against declining volume, selling pressure is diminishing. An upside reaction is imminent.

如交投量下降而價格向下走，顯示沽盤逐漸減弱，升勢可能出現。

11. Should the price go down against increasing open interest and increasing volume, a major downside reaction is imminent. The situation is technically very weak.

如價格向下走，而未平倉合約及交投量均增加，技術走勢極為偏淡，價格可能大幅下跌。

GLOSSARY RELATING TO GOLD
黃金詞滙

Arbitrage

Simultaneous buying and selling of gold in two separate markets in order to exploit price differentials.

套戥

分別在兩個不同的市場同時買入及沽出黃金，以期從價格差異上獲利。

Asked Price

Price at which gold is offered for sale.

賣價

黃金賣家開出的盤價。

Assay

To analyse and determine the fineness of gold.

成色鑑定

分析及確定黃金的純度。

Backwardation

A situation where spot gold price is higher than the gold futures price.

倒價（低息倉費）

現貨金價高於期貨價的情況。

Bear

An individual who perceives that the gold price will fall below the spot level in the future.

淡友

預期金價將會跌至當時水平以下的人。

Bid Price	Price at which an individual is prepared to pay for buying gold.
買價	黃金買家願意付出的價格。
Bull	An individual who perceives that the gold price will rise above the spot level in the future.
好友	預期金價將會升至當時水平以上的人。
Bullion	Gold in non-fabricated form.
金磚	未予加工為製成品的黃金磚。
Bullion Coins	Gold coins minted in large quantities with low (3-5%) selling premium.
金 (磚) 幣	大量鑄造並以較低溢價 (3-5%) 出售的金幣。
Buy at Best	To buy the required quantity of gold at prevailing market price.
不計價買盤	以當時市價購入所需數量的黃金。
Call Option	Option giving the buyer the right but not the obligation to purchase gold at the stated striking price on or before expiration date.
買入期權	給買家選擇在期滿日或之前以指定的行使價購入黃金的權利。

Carat	Unit of the fineness of gold. For example, pure gold is 24 carats and 18 carat gold alloy contains 75% pure gold.
克拉	黃金成色的單位;例如純金為24克拉,而18克拉表示含純金量75%。
Closing Out	Action to close a long or short position.
平倉	買空或賣空的平倉行動。
Contango	A situation where spot gold price is lower than the gold futures price.
順價(高息倉費)	現貨金價低於期貨價的情況。
Collateral	Gold pledged to secure a loan based on the spot price and margin arrangements between the parties concerned.
抵押	有關當事人按現貨價及保證金安排,以黃金為貸款的抵押。
Commission House	An institution which buys and sells gold futures contracts for accounts of their customers.
佣金經紀行	為客戶買賣黃金期貨合約的機構。

Consignment	Gold delivered in advance by a supplier to an agent with the intention to facilitate and increase sales in an overseas market.
託銷貨	供應商為促進及增加在海外市場的銷路而預先交付予代理商的黃金。
Deferred Settlement	Gold purchased or sold to be settled at a later date agreed between the buyer and seller.
遞延結算	黃金交易在買賣雙方協議下在較後日期結算。
Exchange for Physical (EFP)	A situation where the buyer of spot gold transfers to the seller an equivalent number of long gold futures contracts, or vice versa, at an agreed price.
現貨/期貨轉換	現貨黃金的買家按協議的價格將等值的好倉期貨合約轉撥予賣家，或賣家將淡倉合約轉撥予買家。
Fineness	Percentage of pure gold in an alloy expressed as parts per thousand by weight.
成色	合金中所含純金的比率，按重量以千分比表示。

Forward Contract	Contract for settlement of a gold deal at any date later than spot value date.
遠期合約	協議於現貨交收日後任何日期交易結算的黃金合約。
Forward Forward	Simultaneous purchase and sale of gold for different maturity dates in the forward market.
跨期買賣	在遠期市場上同時買賣不同到期日的黃金合約。
Gold Certificate	Document certifying the ownership of gold held at an authorized or recognized depository.
黃金證	證明擁有存放於一獲准或認可保管人的黃金證券。
Gold Futures	Contracts for the purchase or sale of gold for future delivery on a gold futures exchange.
黃金期貨	在黃金期貨交易所買賣未到期交付的黃金合約。
Gold Parity	Officially declared amount of gold to which the currency of a country is equivalent.
黃金官價	官方宣布與該國貨幣單位等值的黃金數量。

Good Delivery Bar	Gold bar which conforms to the specification given by the London Bullion Market Association (LBMA) which is internationally recognized.
國際認許金條	符合倫敦金市協會所訂定國際認可規格的金條。
Gross Weight	The actual weight of a gold bar or coin.
毛重	金條或金幣的實際重量而不是純金重量。
Hedge	Taking a position on a gold futures exchange or on the forward market against a deal concluded on the spot market to protect a profit position.
對沖	在黃金期貨交易所或遠期市場開設對立倉，以保障現貨買賣的利潤。
Hoarding	Accumulation of gold in anticipation of greater value in the future.
囤積	預期金價上升而積存黃金。
Legal Tender	Gold coins which the central bank of a country declares to be acceptable for any payment at their face value.
法定貨幣	一個國家的中央銀行宣稱接受以其面值進行交易的金幣。

Limit Order	Order placed by a customer with a specified limit on either price or time of execution, or both.
限價訂單	指定限價/限期買賣的客戶訂單。
Liquidity	Depth of the market and its ability to absorb large buying or selling orders without wide price fluctuations.
流通量	市場承接大手買賣盤而不致對價格造成大幅波動的容納量。
London Fixing	Setting of the spot gold price which is held at 10:30 hours and 15:00 hours on each working day in the City of London by the five fixing members of the London Bullion Market Association (LBMA).
倫敦議價	於每個工作天的上午10時30分及下午3時由倫敦金市協會五家指定金商在倫敦議定的黃金現貨價。
Margin	The amount of money or collateral deposited with a broker, bank or bullion house to insure against loss on an open position.
保證金（孖展）	存放在經紀行、銀行或金商的款項或抵押品以保障未平倉買賣合約的虧損。

Margin Call	Call for extra deposit as maintenance margin when market moves against an open position held by the customer.
補交保證金通知	當價格上落與客戶未平倉合約背道而行時，要求客戶交付額外保證金以維持原有保證金的水平。
Market Maker	Banks, bullion houses or financial institutions making consistent two-way buy-sell prices for gold.
市場莊家	以雙向價不停作黃金買賣的銀行、金商或金融機構。
Medal	Small gold bar stamped or cast in the shape of a coin having no legal monetary value.
金牌	以黃金鑄造形如硬幣但無法定貨幣價值的小金牌。
One Cancel The Other Order (OCO)	Orders placed by the customer to buy and to sell at specified prices. The sale order will be automatically cancelled when the buy order is filled and vice versa.
自動取消訂單	客戶以指定價格買入或沽出的訂單。一旦買盤完成，賣盤即自動取消，反之亦然。

Open Interest	Total of all open positions on a futures exchange.
未平倉合約	在期貨交易所全部未交收的好倉或淡倉合約。
Put Option	Option giving buyer the right but not the obligation to sell gold at the stated striking price on or before the expiration date.
沽出期權	給買家選擇在期滿日或之前以指定的行使價沽出黃金的權利。
Short Sale	Sale of gold which the seller does not own in anticipation of a lower level of price in the future.
賣空	賣家因預測未來價格會下跌而沽出他並沒有持有的黃金。
Stop Loss Order	Order placed by customer to buy or sell gold at the market if the specified price is reached.
止蝕盤	客戶委託在黃金到達指定價位時在市場上買入或沽出的訂單。

CONVERSION TABLES 換算表

WEIGHT 重量

To Convert 換算：

Ounces troy to grammes 金衡盎司轉克	Multiply by 乘以	31.1035
Grammes to ounces troy 克轉金衡盎司	"	.0321507
Ounces avoirdupois to grammes 常衡盎司轉克	"	28.3495
Grammes to ounces avoirdupois 克轉常衡盎司	"	.0352740
Ounces troy to grains 金衡盎司轉喱	"	480.0
Grains to ounces troy 喱轉金衡盎司	"	.0020833
Ounces troy to ounces avoirdupois 金衡盎司轉常衡盎司	"	1.09714
Ounces avoirdupois to ounces troy 常衡盎司轉金衡盎司	"	.911458
Kilograms to ounces avoirdupois 公斤轉常衡盎司	"	35.2740
Kilograms to ounces troy 公斤轉金衡盎司	"	32.1507
Ounces troy to tolas 金衡盎司轉拖拉	"	2.6667
Tolas to ounces troy 拖拉轉金衡盎司	"	0.375
Kilograms to tolas 公斤轉拖拉	"	85.7550
Ounces troy to taels 金衡盎司轉兩	"	0.83
Taels to ounces troy 兩轉金衡盎司	"	1.20337
Kilograms to taels 公斤轉兩	"	26.7172

LENGTH 長度

To Convert 換算：

Millimetres to inches 毫米轉吋	Multiply by 乘以	.0393701
Inches to millimetres 吋轉毫米	"	25.4
Centimetres to inches 厘米轉吋	"	.393701
Inches to centimetres 吋轉厘米	"	2.54
Metres to inches 米轉吋	"	39.3701
Inches to metres 吋轉米	"	.0254
Feet to metres 呎轉米	"	.3048
Metres to feet 米轉呎	"	3.28084
Yards to metres 碼轉米	"	.9144
Metres to yards 米轉碼	"	1.09361

AREA AND VOLUME 面積及體積

To Convert 換算：

Square inches to square millimetres 平方吋轉平方毫米	Multiply by 乘以	645.16
Square inches to square centimetres 平方吋轉平方厘米	"	6.4516
Square centimetres to square inches 平方厘米轉平方吋	"	.1550
Square millimetres to square inches 平方毫米轉平方吋	"	.00155
Cubic inches to cubic centimetres 立方吋轉立方厘米	"	16.3871
Cubic centimetres to cubic inches 立方厘米轉立方吋	"	.061024

MOST POPULAR KILOBARS IN ASIA 亞洲流通量最高的公斤裝金條

瑞士條

瑞士條

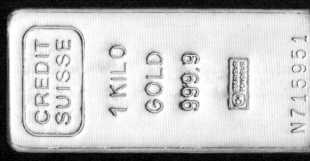

瑞士條

南非條

MOST POPULAR KILOBARS IN ASIA　亞洲流通量最高的公斤裝金條

新加坡條

澳洲條

澳洲條

英國條

ACKNOWLEDGEMENTS 鳴謝

This book was published with the assistance of the Standard Bank Group.

The Standard Bank Group is one of Africa's leading banking and financial services institutions. It has total assets exceeding US$20 billion and currently employs more than 32,000 people. Standard Bank was incorporated in 1862 and the group has now established 1,000 outlets in Africa, Europe, North America and Asia. The acquisition of Ayrton Metals Limited enabled the group to commence the precious metals business in 1994. South Africa is the largest gold producing country in the world and the Standard Bank Group is now actively engaged in the bullion business in major international gold markets in London, New York and Hong Kong.

本書由標旗銀行集團贊助出版。

標旗銀行集團是非洲最大銀行及金融服務機構之一,總資產值超過200億美元,目前聘用32,000多人。標旗銀行於1862年註冊成立,目前在非洲、歐洲、北美洲及亞洲設有1,000間分行。集團於1994年收購雅敦金屬有限公司後開始發展貴金屬業務。南非是世界最大的黃金出產國家,標旗銀行集團現正積極參與倫敦、紐約及香港等主要國際黃金市場的業務。

THANKS ARE ALSO DUE TO 及向下列機構致謝:

Asiaweek, Hong Kong 亞洲週刊 (香港)

Bank for International Settlements, Basle 國際結算銀行 (瑞士)

Bank of England, London 英倫銀行 (倫敦)

Cathay Pacific Airways Limited, Hong Kong 國泰航空有限公司 (香港)

Census and Statistics Department, HK Government, Hong Kong
香港政府統計處 (香港)

Chamber of Mines of South Africa, Johannesburg
南非礦業商會 (約翰內斯堡)

Chinese Gold & Silver Exchange Society, Hong Kong
金銀業貿易場 (香港)

Chow Sang Sang Jewellery Co., Limited, Hong Kong
周生生珠寶金行有限公司 (香港)

Chow Tai Fook Jewellery Co., Limited, Hong Kong
周大福珠寶金行有限公司 (香港)

Continental Jewellery (Mfg.) Limited 恒和珠寶首飾廠有限公司 (香港)

Credit Suisse, Zurich 瑞士信貸銀行 (蘇黎世)

De Beers, Hong Kong 戴比爾斯 (香港)

De Beers Diamond Information Centre, Hong Kong
戴比爾斯鑽石諮詢中心 (香港)

Degussa (Private) Limited, Singapore 迪高沙有限公司 (新加坡)

Deutsche Bank AG, Frankfurt 德意志銀行 (法蘭克福)

Diamond Importers Association, Hong Kong 鑽石入口商會 (香港)

Emphasis (HK) Limited, Hong Kong 安輝斯有限公司 (香港)

Gold Corporation, Australia 澳洲黃金有限公司 (澳洲)

Gold Fields Mineral Services Limited, London
黃金礦業服務有限公司 (倫敦)

Hang Seng Bank, Hong Kong 恒生銀行 (香港)

Hongkong and Shanghai Banking Corporation, Hong Kong
香港上海滙豐銀行 (香港)

HongkongBank Archives, Hong Kong 滙豐銀行檔案室 (香港)

Hong Kong Bullion Dealers Club, Hong Kong
香港黃金交易員協會 (香港)

Hong Kong Dragon Airlines Limited, Hong Kong
港龍航空有限公司 (香港)

Hong Kong Futures Exchange Limited, Hong Kong
香港期貨交易所有限公司 (香港)

Hong Kong Jewellers' and Goldsmiths' Association, Hong Kong
香港珠石玉器金銀首飾業商會 (香港)

Hong Kong Monetary Authority, Hong Kong 香港金融管理局 (香港)

Hong Kong Productivity Council, Hong Kong 香港生產力促進局 (香港)

Hong Kong Tourist Association, Hong Kong 香港旅遊協會 (香港)

Hing Fung Goldsmith & Refinery Limited, Hong Kong
慶豐金鋪有限公司 (香港)

International Monetary Fund, Washington, D. C.
國際貨幣基金會 （華盛頓）

Johnson Matthey plc, London　莊信萬豐有限公司 （倫敦）

Johnson Matthey Hong Kong Limited, Hong Kong
莊信萬豐貴金屬香港有限公司 （香港）

Johnson Matthey Pty Limited, Australia　莊信萬豐有限公司 （澳洲）

Just Gold Co., Limited, Hong Kong　鎮金店有限公司 （香港）

Kummerly + Frey, Switzerland　剛馬利有限公司 （瑞士）

King Fook Gold & Jewellery Co., Limited, Hong Kong
景福金銀珠寶鐘錶有限公司 （香港）

Larry Jewellery Co., Limited, Hong Kong　俊文寶石店 （香港）

Lee Cheong Gold Dealer, Hong Kong　利昌金鋪有限公司 （香港）

London Bullion Market Association, London　倫敦金市協會 （倫敦）

Mase Westpac Hong Kong Limited, Hong Kong
美思太平洋香港有限公司 （香港）

Myer Jewelry Mfr. Limited, Hong Kong　萬雅珠寶有限公司 （香港）

New York Mercantile Exchange, COMEX Division, New York
紐約期貨交易所 （紐約）

Perth Mint, Australia　柏斯鑄幣局 （澳洲）

Po Sang Bank, Hong Kong　寶生銀行 （香港）

Rand Refinery Limited, Johannesburg　南非煉金廠 （南非）

South African Reserve Bank, Pretoria　南非儲備銀行 （比勒陀利亞）

Swiss Bank Corporation, Zurich　瑞士銀行 （蘇黎世）

The Assay Offices, London　黃金成色鑑定局 （倫敦）

The New Airport Projects Co-ordination Office, Hong Kong
新機場工程統籌署 （香港）

The Silver Institute, Washington, D. C.　白銀協會 （華盛頓）

Tse Sui Luen Jewellery Co., Limited, Hong Kong
謝瑞麟珠寶有限公司 （香港）

Union Bank of Switzerland, Zurich　瑞士聯合銀行 （蘇黎世）

World Gold Council, Hong Kong　世界黃金協會 （香港）

INDEX 索引